A Photo Gallery

TUGBOATS
of the Great Lakes

Franz A. VonRiedel

Iconografix

Iconografix
1830A Hanley Road
Hudson, Wisconsin 54016 USA

The information in this book is true and complete to the best of our knowledge. All recommendations are made without any guarantee on the part of the author or Publisher, who also disclaim any liability incurred in connection with the use of this data or specific details.

We acknowledge that certain words, such as model names and designations, mentioned herein are the property of the trademark holder. We use them for purposes of identification only. This is not an official publication.

Iconografix books are offered at a discount when sold in quantity for promotional use. Businesses or organizations seeking details should write to the Marketing Department, Iconografix, at the above address.

Library of Congress Control Number: 2007920343

ISBN-13: 978-1-58388-192-7
ISBN-10: 1-58388-192-1

Reprinted November 2012

Printed in The United States of America

Copyedited by Andy Lindberg

On the cover: Shortly after this book was completed, on December 2, 2006, the author's tug *Seneca* was lost in a huge storm on Lake Superior, 20 miles east of Grand Marais, MI. She is featured on the cover engaged in heavy ice-breaking at Fraser Shipyards in December 2005. The tug was salvaged and raised during Christmas weekend and towed to a Sault Ste. Marie shipyard. The damage is extensive and at the time of this writing, no decision has been made as to the disposition of this classic ship-docking tug. Sadly, this incident probably brought the end for one of the few survivors of the first generation diesel harbor tugs in their original configuration. *Seneca...* we will miss you.

BOOK PROPOSALS

Iconografix is a publishing company specializing in books for transportation enthusiasts. We publish in a number of different areas, including Automobiles, Auto Racing, Buses, Construction Equipment, Emergency Equipment, Farming Equipment, Railroads & Trucks. The Iconografix imprint is constantly growing and expanding into new subject areas.

Authors, editors, and knowledgeable enthusiasts in the field of transportation history are invited to contact the Editorial Department at Iconografix, 1830A Hanley Road, Hudson, WI 54016.

Table of Contents

Dedication

This book is dedicated to a few of my oldest friends, with whom I've been trading research material and photographs for over a decade now. To George Schneider, Bill Moran, Al Hart, Jon LaFontaine, Wendell Wilke, and Jason LaDue... Thanks guys, this one's for you!

Acknowledgements

I would like to express my gratitude to the following people for their invaluable contributions towards this book:

J.O. Bijl, *ST Tugs*, 2006
Al Hart, Bay Village, OH, photography
William A. Hoey, Trenton, MI, operations and vessel research
Jason R. LaDue, Rochester, NY, photography and research
Roger LeLievre, Ann Arbor, MI, *Know Your Ships*, 2006
William Moran, Toronto, Ont, vessel research
Gerry Ouderkirk, Toronto, Ont, photography and research
George R. Schneider, Solana Beach, CA, extensive vessel research
Wade P. Streeter, Detroit, MI, vessel research
Bruce VonRiedel, Knife River, MN, initial proofreading

About The Author

Captain Franz Altman VonRiedel has spent his life documenting the complex histories of the commercial vessels of the maritime industry.

Upon graduation from high school, Franz spent five years working as a conductor on an iron ore railroad. From 1997 – 2000, he restored and operated the *Marine Trader*, the last commercial bumboat in North America.

In 2001, Franz formed the Zenith Tugboat Company, a namesake that paid tribute to Duluth's historic Zenith Dredge Company and the city's old title of "Zenith City." Today Zenith Tug owns and operates five towing vessels.

Franz founded the Northeastern Maritime Historical Foundation in 2002, which has become one of the prime contributors towards the preservation of the towing industry in its history and with the vessels themselves. The Foundation is dedicated to preserving ships and smaller workboats that have contributed to the maritime world in significant ways. Today the Foundation has the world's largest collection of museum tugboats. More information can be found at: www.NortheasternMaritime.org

Besides his time-consuming business interests and hobbies centered around the maritime industry, he is an avid photographer and has had hundreds of images published throughout the United States and Europe. Franz also writes the "North American Update" feature for the bi-monthly magazine, *Lekko International*.

Note: All images in this book were taken by the author unless otherwise credited.

Introduction

Around the world, a once industry standard is quickly becoming a rarity. Many people would refer to this general type of tug as a "dinosaur," but on the Great Lakes, the single screw boat is standard equipment. Single screw, meaning the tug only has one propeller and normally only one engine. No bow thruster, no flanking rudders, no Z-drives, just one big propeller and a lot of horsepower.

In most coastal ports, these tugs have been phased out, with the majority of them having been sent to the bottom for use as artificial reefs or cut up for scrap at local breaking yards. The Lakes contain one of the largest collections of old single screw tugs left operating in the world. Towing volume could never justify the creation of a new harbor tug for Great Lakes service.

Many words could be spent comparing the Lakes to other geographical areas of towage. We could study cargo trends, fleet modernization, increasing ship size (resulting in the decrease of ships) and the lack of tides and other weather factors. But the fact is, the demand just isn't there. Plus, the existing tugs perform just fine.

While modern tugs will be found all throughout these pages, they are far outnumbered on the Lakes by the classic old timers. However well these boats may perform, the day is approaching when they will need to be replaced or once again upgraded. Slowing business and an aging fleet create quite a dilemma. What to do… build new tugs or upgrade the old ones? Doing *either* of those is a tough decision. The industry is far from dying off, it's just spread out over five huge lakes and no single port, with perhaps the exception of Chicago, provides enough action to justify pouring millions of dollars into fleet modernization.

As a vessel owner, I am often discouraged by the ever-increasing burden of Coast Guard regulations. These new requirements forced upon us are costly and for a small operator, can mean the difference between a profitable year or a loss. Then again, so will one marine casualty. However, with tugboats operating in such varied trades, it is nearly impossible to separate them into classes for exemption from certain regulations.

As I write these words, a jacket over my oil-stained pants acts as a table to balance a laptop. I sit in a rickety old lawn chair propped up in the vibrating fiddley of one of these old single screw bombers as we cross a dark, rolling, ice-cold Lake Superior. I can't help but rethink some of my own logic, looking down into the engine room packed with pistons, generators, exciters, relays, knifes, breakers, switches, strainers, chargers, levers, valves and thousands of feet of piping and wiring. I look around and see many changes I'd like to make—many changes we will now be *required* to make. And out in the middle of this darkness, bouncing around in an old harbor tug, I'm glad *someone* regulates this stuff.

At the time of this writing, the times are definitely changing. We are facing the day where the "uninspected towing vessel" will not exist. Soon, all tugs will become inspected and probably for good reason. While this approaches, we wonder, who will take on the inspections, what will they entail and what will it mean for the old fleet of single screw tugs? Will some finally be put to rest, being beyond hope of meeting the new regulations? Will many old classics receive the upgrades required and live on as the survivors they already are? Time will tell.

For now, all across these Great Lakes, the single screw tugs live on.

The famous tug *Record* based at Duluth was one of Captain Inman's boats before the newly formed Great Lakes Towing Company bought his operation. The tug was known to be good in the ice and was built by Globe Shipbuilding at Cleveland in 1884. The iron-hulled tug was retired from the Towing Company in 1927 and sold off-Lakes in 1943 after a brief career with the Couture Brothers Fish Company in Ontonagon, MI. It was repowered to diesel and continued on into the 1970s at Houston, TX. *Author's collection*

Chapter 1
Those Famous "G-Tugs"

The well-known green, red and white harbor tugs, found in every major U.S. port on the Great Lakes, have a colorful history that dates back to the 1800s. These low-profile, single deck tugs with their heavy sheer and sleek lines became known as "G-tugs" early in their career because of the big white "G" on their black smoke stacks.

The G-tugs, as we know them today, were all built by their owner and operator, Great Lakes Towing. The company was formed in 1899 with a buy-out of nearly all the independent harbor tug operators in every port from Duluth to Buffalo. At the time, tugboat service for the ships was in serious need of improvement and out of frustration, many of the steamship and mining company owners formed the

Great Lakes Towing Company, which was incorporated on July 7, 1899. The idea was to consolidate, gain control of the existing harbor tugs and to update the fleet which was long overdue. This was a time of dramatic growth in ship design and technology on the Great Lakes. The old schooners and wooden barges were on the way out. The giant steel "lakers" were on the way in and growing rapidly in size. The old wooden harbor tug fleets could barely keep up.

The firm, which is commonly referred to as "The Towing Company," succeeded in its goal and within a year their fleet amounted to 150 vessels. Some of the early share holders included names such as Mather, Sinclair, Steinbrenner, Hanna, Pickands, Hoyt, Coulby, Rockefeller, and Dunham; virtually

The wooden tug *Fairmount* was built in 1894 at Charlevoix by Joseph Beaubois. The 75-footer wore the name *Ben Campbell* until 1908. It had been acquired from the Cleveland Tug Company during the formation of the Towing Company. The tug was retired and sold in 1911. As the *Fairmount*, it was abandoned at Detroit in 1920. *Photo courtesy of the Northeastern Maritime Historical Foundation*

all the "brand names" of the industry.

Of that early fleet, many of the tugs were immediately retired, never seeing service under Towing Company ownership. With a consolidation of the fleets, the best tugs could be used and stationed in the appropriate areas. Nearly a third of the 150-boat fleet went into lay-up and plans for new construction surfaced almost immediately. The fate of the aging wooden hulled tugs was inevitable. A replacement had to be found.

A need existed for a new powerful steel harbor tug design. A design that could withstand the rapidly changing industry. The present fleet needed to be evaluated, junk tugs sold for scrap and those with life left in them rebuilt for continued service. After an extensive study, the Towing Company began eliminating the old, outdated tugs, often saving their boilers and engines. The wooden tugs took a beating in the harsh conditions of the Great Lakes and were pretty worn out although their machinery was usually in fine condition.

A new design was developed in 1905 that was patterned after the 1897-vintage wooden tug *T. T. Morford*. The new tug would be steel, of course, but was

The G-tug *Florida* (1926) has her steam up and was photographed looking down from a bridge. It seems back in the steam days, tugs had very little fendering on them. The *Florida* is no exception, with only one small bow fender. In line with the cabin, leading back to the quadrant, are guards for her cable steering. The G-tugs, while steam powered, had different smoke stack heights depending on where they were working; the *Florida's* is quite tall. The tug was repowered to diesel in 1955. Thirty years later it was one of the tugs stationed off-Lakes at Tampa. They were renamed for counties in Florida. This tug became the *Pinellas* but its old name was restored upon return to the Lakes in 1985. *Author's collection*

The steamer *Minnesota* is captured in action during spring fit-out. The two steamships have received bottom jobs, with fresh paint on their hulls. On deck of the one ship, the guys are perhaps wondering who will go through the ice first, the tug or their buddy down there getting a little too close! The *Minnesota* was built by the Towing Company in 1911 as Hull No. 14. She was a very powerful tug in her day, powered by a 1000-IHP steeple compound steam engine with 20- and 40-inch cylinders and a 42-inch stroke. The 1896-vintage engine had been removed from the tug *G. A. Tomlinson. Photo courtesy of the Northeastern Maritime Historical Foundation*

similar in appearance. They would be heavily constructed with ice breaking in mind.

The first tug constructed from these new plans was a "Type 1" tug, with dimensions of 73' 4" x 18' 6" x 11'. The boat, named *James R. Sinclair*, was built at the Dunham Towing & Wrecking Company's yard in Chicago. This was a Great Lakes Towing subsidiary. Within months the same yard constructed the first "Type 2" tug. The *Abner C. Harding* was a bit bigger, measuring in at 81' x 20' x 12' 6". In 1907, another Type 1, the *Harvard*, was built at the Buffalo Dry Dock Company. Back in Chicago the following year, another Type 2, the *L. C. Sabin* was built, this being the last tugboat not built at the Towing Company's own shipyard in Cleveland.

In 1909 the *E. M. Pierce* was launched. This was a standard Type 2 tug and completed at a cost of close to $25,000. The tug would later become the *Utah*

and, as a diesel, remained in the Towing Company fleet until 1998 when it was scrapped at Cleveland, only a stone's throw from where it was built almost 90 years earlier.

From this time up until WWI, they built an average of five tugs per year, cranking them out almost in assembly line fashion, replacing the old wooden tugs acquired in the initial formation of the company.

During WW-I, the Shipping Board requisitioned the *Harvey D. Goulder*, *S. C. Schenck*, and the original *Kentucky* (which had been a rename and not a true State-class G-tug). These three steel harbor tugs left the Towing Company for good. A "new" *Kentucky* would be built in 1929.

Through WW-I, steel use was restricted and building slowed. Nevertheless, by 1920 their fleet consisted of 45 new hulls built by the company. A glimpse at the fleet roster that year showed a drastic reduction

Since being repowered with a 12-cylinder 278A Cleveland diesel, the 1200-HP harbor tug *Minnesota* is still alive and well, working from Duluth. She is pictured here on April 5, 2003, at Fraser Shipyards, doing the same work as in the previous photo taken eighty years earlier! Spring fit-out tends to put some rough miles on these hard working little tugs. Heavy ice in the Great Lakes can be a real challenge to penetrate. Once the main channels are broken out by the Coast Guard cutters and the fleets get steam up in their boilers, the harbor tugs start cracking them loose, dragging them out of their lay-up berths for another long season of steady hauling. During her diesel repowering, the *Minnesota*, like most others, received a larger wheelhouse with a rounded front and low engine room trunk, providing far more interior space and better all-around visibility.

of small and out-of-date tugs acquired in the buy-outs of 1899. The fleet had met up with the changing times and now consisted of 60 very capable tugs, stationed throughout the entire Great Lakes system. While many of the old tugs had worn out hulls and auxiliaries, their main engines and sometimes boilers, were in fine condition and removed for future use in newly constructed hulls. This was a pattern into the 1920s and of the 45 home-built tugs on the 1920 roster, only 7 had received new engines and boilers; the remaining all had recycled machinery removed from their predecessors.

The Towing Company, however, had designed a 25" x 28" 750-IHP high-pressure non-condensing single cylinder steam engine to be used in their Type 2 tugs. They also built an 800-IHP 26" x 28" version. Many received this engine, especially the later model tugs of the 1920s and 1930s.

In 1928, the design of the Type 2 tug was modified with a slightly longer hull and various minor changes. The tug *Massachusetts* was the first of the new 84' 4" tugs. With the 1931 completion of the *Idaho*, the tug construction program came to an end. The firm now had a sufficient fleet and the slow times of the 1930s brought no extra demand for towing. General maintenance also suffered during this period and by the time the effects of WW-II hit the Lakes, the steam tugs were not quite up for the challenge. In addition to drastically increased cargos, the newly constructed ships were becoming huge. The days of the 400-foot steamships were numbered and the future appeared to be vessels twice that size. These years were tough on the GLT fleet and after the war the firm decided to look into a major upgrade once again.

The 1947 fleet roster showed a total of 54 tugs, all of them coal-burning steamers. Research on

Why do they call them "G-Tugs"? Since the beginning, the big white "G" on the stacks marked the largest fleet of harbor tugs ever on the Great Lakes. Here we see the standard short stack of the dieselized *Kentucky* in April of 2003. Smoke stack styles varied from the very tall steam type to a shorter river-class steam stack to the streamlined stacks of today, tucked in behind the sleek 1950's rebuilt cabins. The stack housing holds the exhaust piping and mufflers from the single main engine and two diesel generators.

new boilers had been initiated but the idea was dropped when feedback from crews reported much trouble in keeping steam up in the polluted harbor waters, from lack of pure feed water for the boilers. The decision was made to go to diesel power. Working with Mr. Codrington of General Motors, the 12-cylinder model 278A Cleveland diesel became the engine of choice. In 1949, four "test tugs" were completed. The Towing Company gutted the old steamers and removed their cabins. Afterwards, the first two, *Illinois* and *Vermont*, were towed to Bay City to be repowered and reconstructed at DeFoe Boat & Motor Works. At Paasch Marine in Erie, the *Arkansas* and *North Dakota* were converted. After testing, the four tugs became an instant success and a dieselization program was born. Some of the tugs were geared, had Airflex clutches and Falk gearboxes; others had a diesel-electric propulsion system.

During this time of reconstruction, four G-tugs were scrapped but the rest were repowered to diesel. By 1950, their tug *America* was the only one remaining from that original fleet in 1899. That same year, it was decided the *America*, which had been in lay-up at Duluth, would be rebuilt as a lake tug. She received an upper pilothouse. Later, the *Wyoming*,

Idaho, and *Louisiana* would follow with a similar conversion. Since then all have been converted back to low-profile except the *America*, which is still in the fleet today as their *Wisconsin*.

In 1950, four more steamers were converted to diesel at the GLT yard in Cleveland and from then on, the Towing Company did the tug reconstructions "in house." Shortly after completion of those early diesel conversions, a "tug-of-war" took place at Conneaut. The steamers *Minnesota* and *Kentucky* were tied alongside the new diesel tug *North Dakota*, facing the opposite direction. All three tugs worked full ahead and the diesel pulled the two steamers backwards. Many say it was staged for publicity since steam power is virtually unlimited. The steamers did the job, but the fact was, the machinery was nearing the point of being ancient and times were changing.

The dieselization program was a great success, with drastic reductions in pollution and operating costs and an equally noticeable increase in maneuverability and efficiency. The rebuild cost averaged $165,000 per tug.

Another style emerged from the old G-tugs. The *Maine*-Class retained their "high back" deckhouse which houses a galley, shower, and head. These tugs, the *Maine, Maryland, Oregon,* and *Michigan* were intended for lake towing, providing the necessities for a short-term live-on crew. Today, only one high-back tug remains in the Towing Company fleet and that is the *Maine*. Interestingly, the *Oregon* and *Michigan* also exist, but are in the hands of competing tug companies.

During the prime of their repowering program, on November 1, 1952, the highly polluted Cuyahoga River in Cleveland caught fire. As it swept towards the Towing Company shipyard, the steam tugs *Arizona* (waiting to be repowered), *Wyoming* (stripped for repowering), and the *Michigan* (with a nearly completed conversion) were sitting ducks. The fire destroyed the GLT yard and severely damaged all three tugboats. The *Michigan* was a total loss, setting her repowering back to the beginning. This fire brought the rebuild program to a grinding halt as the firm recovered and repaired their shipyard.

The fleet of 1200-HP diesel G-tugs received new cabins, consisting of merely a small engine room trunk and a larger pilothouse with better all-around visibility. Today these powerful little tugs still make up the bulk of the ship-assist tug fleets around the

The 1928-vintage *Massachusetts* is getting a line on the bow of the steamer *Sylvania* in preparation for sailing. Much like the tugboat that is about to assist her, the *Sylvania* lasted a long life of nearly eighty years in the fresh waters of the Great Lakes. Having suffered countless groundings, multiple collisions, fires, and even a sinking, the 1905 steamship kept on ticking until finally being scrapped in 1984. With proper maintenance, the steel hulls tend to last "forever" in this environment. *Author's collection*

Lakes. An afterthought improvement led to the installation of steerable kort nozzles on many of the tugs. The Towing Company was the first operator in the United States to use such an arrangement.

As the years went on, some of the G-tugs were again repowered and today a number of them have either 567C or 645E model EMD engines. The EMD engines have been found to last quite a bit longer than the Clevelands, in terms of rebuild hours. Both were General Motors products, but the Cleveland diesel division closed and the EMDs continued. They are still a popular choice for tugboat power in newly constructed vessels today.

Very few dieselized G-tugs have ever found their way out of the Towing Company's hands. In 1978, two Maine-Class tugs, the *Oregon* and *Michigan* were sold to Seaway Towing at Sault Ste. Marie, which was at the time not territory of the Towing Company. After a few years, the tugs were resold to North American Towing and brought to Duluth as the *Sioux* and *Dakota*, working in direct competition with GLT until 1991. North American shut down

Compare to the previous photo; seventy-eight years after her construction, the Towing Company's Hull No. 58 is still going strong. Behind the *Massachusetts* and fleetmate *Arizona*, the 1000-footer *Burns Harbor* unloads taconite pellets at its namesake, the Port of Burns Harbor. Her cargo of roughly 55,000-tons would have been loaded a few days earlier at the Burlington Northern No. 5 ore dock in Allouez on Lake Superior. The fast loading and unloading of modern day Lakeboats deliver the pellets to the mills often still warm from the processing plants.

and the tugs were placed in lay-up at Chicago. In the late 1990s, Selvick purchased the *Dakota* and today it is in service at Green Bay. In 2004, Zenith Tug bought the *Sioux* and it returned to Duluth, where it also is back in service.

Typically, and for good reason, upon retirement the G-tugs are stripped and cut up for scrap. The fleet tugs, being nearly identical, provide a tremendous parts source. Also, scrapping eliminates the concern of helping a competitor.

In 1984, the Type 2 tug *Missouri* was renamed *Michigan*, keeping the tug names in states they served. The *Michigan* and sister tug *New Mexico* left the Lakes in 1997 and were restationed at Puerto Rico, still owned and operated by Great Lakes Towing. The *New Mexico* had been built in 1910 but immediately let out on lease to the Pere Marquette Railway and named *W. L. Mercereau*, honoring the railway's marine superintendent. At Puerto Rico, the *Michigan* was renamed *Punta Tuna* and the *New Mexico* was named *Punta Lima*. After five years, the contract they were needed for came to an end and the tugs were retired. Today, the *Tuna* is owned by a ship-docking firm in St. Thomas and working under the name *Superior*. The *Lima* was sold to an operator in the Dominican Republic and was last spotted in lay-up at the Santo Domingo shipyard.

Over the years, several G-tugs have left the Lakes bound for special projects but would all return home upon completion of their mission. In the spring of 1983, the *Maine*, *Maryland*, *Florida*, and *Missouri* all went down to Tampa for a season. They returned to the Lakes the following year. In 1986, the *Wyoming*, *Nebraska*, *Tennessee*, *Pennsylvania* and *Maine* went down to Florida for a Naval contract at Pensacola. Through the first year, the *Wyoming* and *Nebraska* were in Cape Canaveral but later joined their sisters on the Gulf side. They returned to the Lakes in 1995.

Tugs have also been stationed on charter in Charleston and wore the McAllister Towing colors on their smoke stacks. Reports from the crews who ran them off-Lakes indicated they immediately fell in love with the handy G-tugs. Small in size, compared to the monster salt-water tugs, they offered better maneuverability and still plenty of torque for moving the large ships. Also their low-profile design allows for unlimited access to the ship's hull, such as getting up under the bow flare when docking or undocking.

As the years go by another fleet upgrade, possibly a new tug design all-together, is inevitable. It will be interesting to see what the future holds. However, for now, the ubiquitous G-tugs are still going strong and should be around to watch for decades to come.

January 27, 1998, at the Great Lakes Towing Company's shipyard in Cleveland. The tug *Arkansas* is laid up temporarily for an overhaul. One of the oldest in the fleet today, she began life in 1909 as the *Yale* and was one of the first to be repowered to diesel. This occurred in 1949 at which time Towing Company's Hull No. 8 was given her present name. Behind her in the drydock, the *Virginia* is visible and receiving new paint and repairs to her rudder and wheel. *Yale's* original engine was an 1888-built Sutton Brothers 23" x 28" 500-IHP steam engine that had been salvaged out of the tug *S. W. Gee.* It was repowered with a 12-278A Cleveland diesel.

It's the beginning of the 2003 shipping season and the 1910-vintage tug *North Dakota* (Hull No. 11) is bashing her way through the solid, thick ice that has formed inside the Fraser Shipyards in Superior, WI. The wall of steel behind her is the hull of the steamer *Reserve*, a 750-foot Laker built in 1953. The *North Dakota* was originally named *John M. Truby* but given its present name in 1938. She will run ahead until stalling out, riding up and becoming stuck in the hard ice. Running the wheel to blow the broken ice away from her stern, the tug will then carefully back down in the track she just cut. Once some open water is ahead of her, she charges ahead again, backing and ramming until the ice is all broken, as ordered by their customer. This process can be brutal on the hulls.

The freshly painted *Indiana* (Hull No. 15, built in 1911) and *Texas* (Hull No. 41, built in 1916) rest at their home pier under a bridge in Green Bay. The tugs are not used often in this port. The Towing Company provides a Lakes-wide service covering nearly every port on the Lakes. The busier harbors tend to subsidize the low-volume ports like Green Bay and Buffalo for example. The *Indiana* was built by GLT but originally owned by its subsidiary Dunham Towing & Wrecking of Chicago. The tug was on the scene after the passenger vessel *Eastland* capsized on July 24, 1915. The *Indiana* and sister tugs *Racine* and *Kenosha* assisted in saving many lives.

The *Pennsylvania* was Hull No. 16, built at Great Lakes Towing in 1911. It was built with a single cylinder, 25-inch bore by 28-inch stroke, high pressure, non-condensing 750-IHP steam engine. This was the first tug to receive this type of engine, which was designed and built by the Towing Company themselves. The same engine would be used in many more tugs being repowered or built new, the last one being the *Idaho*, constructed in 1931. In this photo, the *Pennsy* is boarded up tight for a tow to the Cleveland shipyard. She is powered by an 8-498 Cleveland with a 4:1 Falk gear and slip clutch.

In this June 1996 image, the *New York* and *Arizona* are stationed in South Chicago at the Towing Company's yard near 92nd Street. The *New York* (Hull No. 23) was built in 1913 and wasn't repowered until 1960, being one of the last to still operate under steam power. The *Arizona* (Hull No. 66) came to life in 1931. The stack is set towards the back of the engine room trunk allowing for a large open area that once held a retractable hydraulic boom that held an operating cab (phone-booth type pilothouse). This "sky-pilot" unit could be raised and lowered and moved side to side to allow the ultimate visibility for moving barges in the river system and mills of lower Lake Michigan. This experimental set-up was short-lived and eventually uninstalled.

The 1914-built *Vermont* (Hull No. 28) is pictured on October 31, 1996, in the Duluth harbor turning the ocean-going freighter *Federal Fraser*. With the *Minnesota* working the bow, the two tugs pulled the ship out from the AGP Cap. 6 grain elevator. They are spinning it around in the harbor before re-docking the vessel in the same berth, backwards, to finish loading of its cargo bound for an overseas country. Her original 23" x 28" steam engine was replaced with a Cleveland diesel as part of the first group to go through the repowering program in 1949.

At Erie, PA, the tugs *Iowa* (Hull No. 35, 1915) and *Rhode Island* (Hull No. 65, 1930) rest between jobs on March 16, 1997. Both are Type 2 tugs, but the *Iowa* is 81' long while the *Rhode Island* is a tad larger at 84' 4". This slight design modification took place in 1928 with virtually no difference in appearance.

The *Missouri* and *Utah* are heading out to dock a ship in this 1970s photo. The *Missouri* and sister *New Mexico* were taken off-Lakes in 1997 for use in Puerto Rico. Puerto Rico Towing & Barge Company, a Great Lakes Towing subsidiary, used them at the Naval yard until 2002 when the contract ended. In this image, unusual bow fendering can be found on the *Missouri*. Rubber is mounted from the waterline up, useful for pushing vessels with minimal freeboard, such as loaded barges. The typical G-tug bow fender can be found on the tug *Utah*, in the background. *Author's collection*

The tugs are rotated between ports, eventually all finding their way back to the Cleveland shipyard for major repair and upgrades. The *Texas* and *Indiana* were stationed at Erie in this 1994 image. A decade later, the pair would still be teamed up, but this time at Green Bay, WI. The tugs are sporting white canvas over their bow fenders to protect the U.S. Navy ship they just docked from blemishes caused by the black rubber fendering. This is commonly required by Naval vessels, passenger ships and anyone else who does not care to have their pretty little hulls scuffed up by a dirty old tugboat.

It is January 1998 and at Buffalo the tugs are almost finished for the season. The Steinbrenner ship *Kinsman Independent* is wintering at the grain elevator across the river. Crews are busy putting both the ship and the tugs to bed for winter. The *New Jersey* (Hull No. 51, 1924) and *Mississippi* (Hull No. 42, 1916) were stationed in the port at the time. The *Mississippi* was originally powered with the 350-IHP fore and aft compound engine removed from the wooden tug *Zenith.* It was repowered in 1957 with a 12-278A Cleveland diesel-powered DC generator with an electric drive unit. The *New Jersey* has the same engine but with a gearbox.

At the Towing Company's Cleveland shipyard, retired tugs are kept on hand as a source for parts. In this June 3, 2004, image, the *Tennessee* and *Alabama* have seen better days. If you know where to look, the *Tennessee* has several loose brackets and flanges where piping for two big fire monitors were once mounted. This tug was one of five that served in Pensacola, FL from 1986 through May of 1995 as part of a Naval contract. It has been outfitted with grey, Navy D-rubber all down her rub-rail. The tug was repowered in 1960 with a 1400-HP Cleveland 8-498. The electric *Alabama* is likely the tug to be laid up the longest now in the G-tug fleet and will most likely never see service again. *Al Hart photo*

The Towing Company's Hull No. 44 was completed in 1917 at Cleveland and became the State tug *Louisiana*. Today she is stationed at Toledo and is powered by the standard 12-278A Cleveland diesel. In the late 1980s, due to improper lay-up, the *Arkansas* sank at Duluth. She took the *Louisiana*, which had been rafted alongside, down with her. The pair were raised and towed to Cleveland for repair.

On April 11, 2002, the 1924 electric tug *Delaware* (Hull No. 50) tows the *Maumee* stern-first on the Cuyahoga River downtown Cleveland. The *Maumee* is operated by Grand River Navigation, a subsidiary of Lower Lakes Towing, who is one of GLT's best customers at the busy port of Cleveland. The firm operates a large fleet of classic lakeboats. *Al Hart photo*

The *California* is another G-Tug with an electric propulsion system. These 900-HP tugs are said to be a little on the tired side and are slowly being phased out as most engineers favor the gear driven tugs. There are more diesel-electric tugs still in service on the Great Lakes than anywhere else in the world. Hull No. 54, built in 1926, is pictured in Milwaukee on July 25, 1993. The tug has since been relocated to Cleveland and the G-tug dock in this photo is now all built up with condos and would hardly be recognizable.

The poor old *Connecticut* (Hull No. 56, built in 1927) rests along the banks of the Cuyahoga River in April 1997. Having spent her final few years in lay-up, the tug was used for a parts source and finally, in 1998, sold for scrap. Sister tugs *Nevada* (Hull No. 64, built in 1930) and *Utah* (Hull No. 7, built in 1933) and the big lake tug *Georgia* (1916) were all scrapped at the same time. The *Connecticut* was first to go under the knife and the *Nevada* followed. The scrapping happened just across the river from the location of this photo. It can be noted in the image her bow tow-bitt, life raft, nav lights and all fendering have been removed. Probably still containing some decent engine parts, her stack is kept tarped in case the company wants to salvage any more before she is broken up. *Al Hart photo*

The *Montana* (Hull No. 60, built in 1929) was rebuilt with a 1400-HP 8-cylinder 498 Cleveland diesel generator in 1956. A large DC propulsion motor turns an 8' 6" diameter propeller through a 4.233:1 Farrel reduction gear. Her green paint has worn off the bow from rubbing in the ice and her primer coat is showing in this photo. The tug is heading out to help a ship from its berth. On top of the engine room trunk, an orange canister-type inflatable life raft is mounted in a cradle. This is standard equipment on most tugboats, a safety feature that gives its crew peace of mind when offshore.

Spring thaw is upon us but cold temperatures at night form icicles on the 1929 tug *Nebraska* (Hull No. 61) as she lies at GLT's South Chicago facility on March 15, 1997. She is fitted with grey Navy fendering bow to stern, left over from her time spent in Florida docking Navy ships. She was repowered with a 1450-HP EMD 12-645-E6 engine in 1980 and along with sister tug *Wyoming* are among the finest in the fleet. The tug just ahead of the *Nebraska* in this image has an unusual tow-bar addition to its stern. A feature commonly found, in much larger form, on ocean-going tugs to keep the towline from chaffing on the stern of the tug.

At Duluth, March 24, 2005, the *Kentucky* (Hull No. 63, built in 1929) guides a Canada Steamship Lines self-unloader down the Front Channel. The tugs run out ahead and loosen all the ice from the harbor entrance to whichever dock the ship is bound. Afterwards, they meet the ship on arrival and guide them to their berth. The *Kentucky* is sitting down in the bow due to ballasting. The engineer can divert the tug's cooling water to flood the 5,000-gallon circulation tank, lowering the bow. This is needed for ice-breaking. The same compartment can be emptied with ease by turning a couple valves and again use the main engine's cooling water pumps to discharge the tank. Running the cooling water off this tank while working in ice will help prevent loss of suction from plugged strainers and sea-chests.

At Burns Harbor, the *Arizona* is stationed and provides ship assistance to ships visiting the port. A modern pilothouse, smoke stack and deck winches are an interesting contrast to the ancient riveted hull plate and classic bow and stern tow-bitts that date back to the turn of the century. The deck winches mounted on the bow are a rare sight on a G-Tug. The *Arizona*, as noted in an earlier caption, was once outfitted for barge service in the Chicago area. The winches would have been used for facing wires to hook-up barges when pushing ahead. The tug is powered by an EMD 12-567C with a Falk horizontal offset reduction gear.

The *Rhode Island* is standing by below the bow of a U.S. Steel freighter at the Duluth, Missabe & Iron Range Railway ore docks in West Duluth. The tugs usually require several hours call-out notice. Often times the estimated departure time will change by the time the tug arrives and the crews will patiently wait, "on the clock," of course. Once the ship is ready, the crew of the *Rhode Island* will take a line off their bow and help steer the loaded ship backing out of its berth and then line them up for the channel. The fellow on deck is standing by an opening in the "trunk" directly in front of the pilothouse. Through this opening, a set of stairs will lead to the forecastle area, usually home to several bunks. Nothing fancy, this make-shift crew accommodations area is more often a nice heated area to stow towing gear, keeping it dry and out of the way.

The Type 2 tug *Q. A. Gillmore* was built in 1913 as Hull No. 24. Her engine was salvaged out of the large wooden tug *Monarch*. It was a 450-IHP fore and aft compound, built in 1884. However, speculation exists that it was originally a single cylinder engine built in 1873 but professionally reconstructed by the S. F. Hodge Company at Detroit, hence the 1884 build date. The vessel was sold as surplus in 1932 for $22,000 to the C. Reiss Coal Company. They ran the *Gillmore* one year before renaming the vessel *Reiss*. The tug was stationed at Green Bay to dock Reiss ships. Owned by a coal company, they had no reason to convert her to oil or diesel and today she remains a coal-fired steamer with her original engine. In 1969, the Reiss Steamship Company was sold to American Steamship. The same year, Mr. R. J. Peterson purchased this classic tug for $7,000. His crew ran it across Lake Michigan under its own power to its new museum berth in Saugatuck. The tug was fired and run at the dock periodically into the 1980s.

This unusual view is looking inside the water drum on the lower end of the *Gillmore's* 200-PSI Foster Wheeler Type 'A' water tube boiler. Water flows inside the tubes and the hot gases flow outside. When a tube fails, a brass plug can be used to close off the one bad tube until it can be replaced. In this photo, a plug is visible on the lower right side. The tubes run diagonally from a water drum on each side up to the steam drum in the top center of the boiler. Originally she was constructed with a fire-tube boiler. This was replaced shortly after the sale to Reiss.

The *Gillmore's* 2-cylinder steam engine stands two stories tall. The 1884 engine, to this day, is in immaculate condition. Her 30-inch diameter low-pressure cylinder is astern, on the left, and to the right is her 16-inch high-pressure cylinder. The engine has a stroke of 28-inches. This view from the fiddley area shows the cylinder block and engine controls. The tug is in immaculate condition but is overdue for dry-docking and boiler repair. In 2004, the tug was donated to the Northeastern Maritime Historical Foundation and the name *Q. A. Gillmore* was restored. As the last steam G-tug in the world, the long-term goal of the Foundation is to make her once again operable.

At South Chicago, one of the last dock facilities still owned by GLT, the *Maryland* (Hull No. 53, built in 1925) is a prime example of a "high back" diesel G-Tug. Only a handful of the converted G-Tugs were left with their tall aft cabin from the steam days. This space allowed the tug a fiddley area, head, shower, and galley in the stern. In 1998, while stationed at Burns Harbor, the *Maryland* took a beating during a heavy blow on the lake. After being bashed against the dock repeatedly by the massive swells, the tug eventually split open, took on water and sank at the dock. The boat was raised and dismantled for scrap. In this image, the tug has a white stripe painted low on her bow. This is a water mark often used when towing deadship. The tug had likely just returned from repairs in Cleveland. The crew on the towing tug can look back and, even in fog or a heavy sea, tell by measuring the waterline to this white mark if the tug is still safe, towing well and not taking on water. In this December 1995 image, the fleet is laid-up and their spotlights and radars are wrapped with plastic bags and duct tape for the winter months.

Upbound through the Soo Locks in September 1961 is the tug *Maine* (Hull No. 49, built in 1921). She is the last remaining G-Tug in the fleet with the high back cabin. These tugs were useful for overnight jobs where some basic accommodations were needed. Today the classic lifeboats, as seen in this image, have all been replaced with canister type life-rafts. It is also interesting to note the tires, which the Towing Company does not often use for fendering. The tug was repowered in the 1950s with a 12-567A and in 1966 received a C-block 567. Originally, the tug had the standard 25" x 28" Towing Company steam engine. *Author's collection*

Two other high aft cabin tugs were the *Michigan* (Hull No. 26, built in 1913) and *Oregon* (Hull No. 48, built in 1921). In an extremely rare move on the Towing Company's part, the two tugs were sold to a non-competing tug company at the Soo in 1978. However, only three years later they were resold and found working against GLT in direct competition at Duluth under the names *Dakota* and *Sioux*, respectively. In this 1998 image, the tugs are in lay-up at Chicago after their operator went out of business. Renamed *Ethel E.* and *Susan E.*, the tugs are in Egan Marine colors and awaiting their fate, which at this point does not appear too promising. Behind them is the tug *Stamina*, built in 1931 and still powered by a 200-HP, 4-Cylinder C-Model Kahlenberg oil engine.

As the years went on, the two stray high-backs were passed through several owners and at the time of this writing are once again in direct competition with the Towing Company. The *Michigan*, renamed *St. Marie II* in 1978, *Dakota* in 1981, and *Ethel E.* in 1992, was sold by Egan Marine to John Selvick, who used it briefly in Chicago before selling it to his sister's operation in Sturgeon Bay. Now named *Jacquelyn Nicole*, the boat is pictured at Green Bay on May 14, 2005. It is powered by a 1200-HP EMD 12-567A engine which turns a 9-inch shaft through a Falk gearbox. The tug is owned by Selvick Marine Towing and used in the ship-docking trade at Green Bay and Marinette.

In the late 1980s at the Duluth Port Authority, the *Sioux* and *Dakota* are laid up for winter. The pair arrived in the port on September 1, 1981, and for ten years gave Great Lakes Towing a good run for their money. Their owner, North American Towing, went under in 1991 and all seven of the firm's tugs were taken to Chicago for an extended lay-up.

Resting in the Zenith Tug yard, the former *Susan E.* was purchased from Hannah late in 2004 and brought "home" to Duluth. For twelve years the tug had been laying, unused, in South Chicago. Her former North American name, *Sioux*, was restored and the tug was given a complete overhaul, as pictured in this August 2005 photo.

Overhaul complete, in September 2005 the *Sioux* returned to service. In this November photo, she is busting ice down the Missabe cross-channel in anticipation of the steamer *Arthur M. Anderson's* arrival. As the G-tug *Oregon*, it assisted another tug, the *America*, freeing the grounded steamer *B. F. Jones* on October 23, 1941. The *Oregon* was pulling on the *America*, which was pulling on the *Jones*. The *America*, being in the middle, fell victim to an unusual reaction to its torque, flipping the tug over between the *Oregon* and the *Jones*, killing six of her crew members. *Sam Lapinski photo.*

This image, taken at the Detroit tug dock near the Jefferson Avenue Bridge, is a perfect example of how the steam powered G-tugs, although identical hulls, had smoke-stacks of various heights. Here, the *Oregon* and *Minnesota* are shown together near the small wooden G-tug office with the name proudly displayed across the front. *Author's collection*

Sixty years later, the same two tugs are still in operation, now powered by diesel engines and stationed in Duluth. Passing the *Minnesota* and *North Dakota*, the competing *Sioux* was formerly the G-tug *Oregon*. Variations can be found among all G-tugs, but besides a slight difference in the color of their green hulls, the identical tugs pictured all date back to the early 20th century as Type 2 steam tugs.

It's June 2005 and, under a setting sun, the *Sioux* has just cleared Whitefish Bay and is heading home to Duluth. The machinery's running fine and it's a beautiful night on a calm Lake Superior. No better place to be! It may seem like driving a tank, trying to see over the heavy sheer and massive bow of a G-tug. But as ship-docking tugs, they're built like that for a reason.

The former City-Class tug *Buffalo* rests at Fraser Shipyards in this May 1991 image. Under the name *Rueben Johnson*, the tug was retired from service in the mid-1990s, joining six other unused shipyard tugs lying around the yard. Built as Hull No. 19 for the Towing Company, it was sold for $30,000 in 1928 to the U.S. Army Corps of Engineers and renamed *Churchill*. After WW-II, it was sold to Boland & Cornelius and put to work at Sodus Point, NY assisting their own ships. It was retired from service in 1965 and with fresh B&C paint she departed Sodus on July 12th. Ten days later the tug's crew caught a line on the dock of her new owner, the Fraser-Nelson Shipyard in Superior. *Jon LaFontaine photo*

Today the *Reuben Johnson* retains much of its original interior and is in fairly decent condition for a vessel nearing 100 years old. Her original steam power plant was removed at Erie, PA in 1955 and replaced with a pair of 6-110 Detroit diesels to a single screw. The tug has been out of service for a good ten years now. Hopefully one day the tug will be preserved. It would be a shame to see such a fine example of the Type 1 G-Tug sent to the scrapyard.

No longer in service, the tug *Alaska* is moored at the G&W dock in Cleveland with the larger Type 2 tug *Alabama*. The City-Class tug *Alaska* was the only one to ever receive a State name. Launched in 1912 as the *Gary*, the tug was sold to the C. Reiss Coal Company in 1934 for service docking its own ships on Lake Michigan. Appropriately enough, she was given another city name, *Green Bay*. Interestingly, the tug was reacquired by Great Lakes in 1990 and given her state name. In 1999 it was sold off-Lakes along with two former Gaelic tugs acquired in a buy-out. The two Gaelic boats continued on through the Erie Canal in 2000 but while there the *Alaska* was left behind as the owner realized the vessel was ancient and virtually worthless in commercial service.

In 1957, the *Green Bay* was repowered with a Kahlenberg E-6 engine, one of only six built. Today this engine, serial # 603, is the only one left (with the exception of one put on display at the Wisconsin Maritime Museum at Manitowoc). Many say the E-6 was one of the finest engines ever built. Too good, in fact. So good that nobody would pay the premium for quality. The engine that cost them $90,000 to build would only sell for $60,000, which was still roughly twice the price of a new EMD. With the ten years of research and development, the proposition nearly bankrupted the company. As always with the Kahlenberg family, quality always came first. Today the firm is a leader in marine air horns for workboats of all sizes including large freighters.

One of the nicest things about photographing G-tugs in their homeport of Cleveland is the ability to capture the Terminal Tower in the background from nearly any location around the port. The beautiful Terminal Tower, just above the tug's aft quarter in this image, has been home to the Towing Company's corporate headquarters since 1929. The City-Class tug *Ashtabula* is privately owned in this June 2004 photo. The tug had been sold into Canadian ownership years ago and after an extended lay-up at Windsor as the *Jenny T. II*, the tug was rescued from the boneyard in 2002. The *Ashtabula* was built in 1915 and served the Towing Company for thirty years before it was sold to Harry Dixon of Toronto.

Powered by a model EV-5MG 8-cylinder turbocharged 430-HP Lister-Blackstone diesel, the *Ashtabula* is typical of the City-Class tugs that escaped GLT ownership. Typical in that most of the tugs received unique conversions, including unusual engines. Sadly, in June of 2006, while undergoing repairs, a spark from some hot work ignited a fire which destroyed the vessel, leaving the forward end a true mess. At the time of this writing, no decision had been made as to the vessel's disposition. Originally the tug was powered by a recycled steam engine which was taken from the tug *Chris Grover*. The wooden *Grover* was similar in size and junked in 1914, at which time its engine was saved for future use.

The *Stephen M. Selvick* is ready to be scuttled as a dive attraction in Munising Bay. A few days after this photo was taken in December 1995, the tug sank a little ahead of schedule in shallow water. Crews dewatered the tug and come spring, it was intentionally scuttled on the appropriate site, in 60-feet of water. The tug was originally the City-Class tug *Lorain*, built in 1915 at Great Lakes Towing. It was requisitioned by the Navy and became the *YTM-330* in the 1940s. In 1948, the tug was purchased by the Merritt, Chapman & Scott Corporation and used in construction of the Mackinaw Bridge under the name *Cabot*. Selvick purchased the tug in 1974 and operated it at Sturgeon Bay. It was donated in the early 1990s to the Alger Underwater Preserve.

Another City-Class tug, which had received substantial structural modifications, is the 1914 *Fairport*. Sold during WW-II to Canada Steamship Lines, the tug was later repowered to diesel after a 1959 sinking. Given a new cabin and modified stern, today the vessel shows little evidence of her Towing Company heritage. The engine and towing machine have since been removed and put to use in the Purvis tug *Adanac*. Today, the old *Fairport*, under the name *Rod McLean*, rests in the boneyard portion of Purvis Marine's yard above the Canadian Soo Locks.

The tug *America* is in action in the Duluth harbor. On April 23, 1906, the tug put out a fire on the Northern Pacific Railway's west draw of the St Louis River Bridge. A letter dated May 4, 1906, addressed to Capt. H. E. Ditzel of the *America*, thanked the skipper and his crew for their "neighborly act." Oddly, the letter was written by Vice President McGonagle of the DM & N Railway, "per request of the Northern Pacific." Perhaps the N.P. had run out of stationary. The 90-foot tug was Hull No. 81 of the Union Dry Dock Company at Buffalo. The riveted steel hull was built with an H. G. Trout fore and aft 16 and 32" x 28" 490-IHP steam engine. *Author's collection*

The tug *America* ended up mothballed in Duluth and eventually she was taken to the Cleveland yard for an overhaul. She was given an upper pilothouse for service in lake towing and barge work. The steamer re-entered service in 1941 but only a few weeks into her revitalized career, the tug met with disaster. On October 23rd, the tug was assisting the grounded laker *B. F. Jones* in the Detroit River when it suddenly capsized. Six of her crewmembers lost their lives. The tug was raised and later rebuilt again, this time to diesel. In 1983, it was given the state name *Wisconsin*.

The *Wisconsin* is powered by a 1200-HP EMD 12-567C engine. On the front, its governor is visible in the top center and just to the right is the fuel pump. Fuel oil manifolds are on each side below the top deck, along with a set of fuel filters on the left side. Two large pipes rise out of the bilge, leading to the water pump. Below the exhaust manifold are three long covers protecting the top deck of the engine from debris. Under those covers are the cylinder heads, injectors, rocker arms, camshaft, jumper lines, valves, and all those type of goodies. While shut down, the oil drains out of these engines, lying on the bottom. Before a start, they need to be pre-lubed by opening two valves, routing the oil through an auxiliary lube-oil pump which builds oil pressure. With a top deck cover off, you watch for oil running out of the bearings. Once oil is up top again, the pump is shut off, valves closed and the engine is ready to be turned over. Down the side of the block,

in line with the fuel filters in this photo, are six test cocks. These need to be opened prior to starting. Once the engine is pre-lubed and air is up, the engine is spun over without starting to blow any condensation or water out. Once the engine is "blown down," you close the test cocks, wait for air to build up again and then start the engine. Getting a cold tugboat up and running normally takes about 45 minutes. You don't just turn a key. These 567s are, at least in my humble opinion, about the best engine ever built. They are powerful, fuel efficient, quiet, have readily available parts, and are easy to work on; more or less just an overgrown Detroit 71. Unfortunately, the days of the old 2-stroke medium speed diesels are about over. Production of the 567 engine ended in 1966 after thirty years of building these beautiful engines in A-, B-, C-, and D-block styles.

Like all G-tugs, the *Wisconsin* is steered with a stick rather than a wheel. They have throttle stands on both sides, one live and the other a repeater. This way, the captain can work from either side of the house. In the front center, there is a "dash" with a compass and pressure gauges showing forward and reverse clutch air. Today, the *Wisconsin* lives on as the only surviving member of the original G-tug fleet, acquired in the 1899 formation of the Great Lakes Towing Company.

The Gaelic dock in Detroit has been the home to many of the 88-foot Alexander tugs. Here, the 1951 *Carolyn Hoey* waits between jobs with fleetmate *Roger Stahl*, a former Coast Guard 110-foot WYTM-class ice-breaking tug. The *Carolyn* was the former *Atlas*, a name she wore until a purchase and total rebuild by Gaelic Tug in 1984. Like most of them, it was originally powered by an LST-surplus 567A. That engine was removed in the late 1960s when a 16-278A Cleveland replaced it. In 1987 the tug was repowered again, this time with a 16-567C EMD engine. Her pilothouse has also been replaced with something a little more user-friendly, providing excellent all-around visibility for ship-assistance duties on the Rouge River.

Chapter 2
Harbor Tugs: Ship Assistance

In addition to the large fleet of G-tugs situated throughout the Lakes, an even larger fleet of tugs exist that are owned and operated by independent tug companies. They provide the same ship-assist service in most ports on the U.S. and Canadian side of the Lakes. While their customers are not obligated to signing a lakes-wide contract, they receive the same professional tug service when using these independents, often at a lesser rate due to the low-overhead of the "Ma and Pa" operations.

The major competitor for these companies is, of course, Great Lakes Towing. The company was formed in 1899 with the intention of eliminating all competition and 110 years later still operates under the same philosophy. However, the effect is more historical than intentional. They provide a reliable service and many of their founding father's heirs still have loyalty to that firm.

Other ship assistance tug companies certainly exist and each time a piece of work is handed to these

It's June 2001 and time for the annual Detroit River tugboat races. After the race excitement ends, the party begins! The tugs all raft in at Windsor's Dieppe Park for the awards ceremony and lunch. The starting line is near the Essroc Silos west of the Ambassador Bridge and the tugs run upriver to the finish line near the above-mentioned park. It is not uncommon to see the bright, clean, green and white tugs of the Gaelic fleet take the top positions in the race. Here, the *Patricia Hoey*, *Shannon*, and *Roger Stahl* are moored alongside each other while the crews pick up their awards. The *Shannon* began life in 1944 as the *USS Connewango YTB-338*. The tug's owner, Capt. Bill Hoey, had its smoke stack partially repainted to pay tribute to her Naval history, which is clearly visible in this photo and appreciated by the thousands of often over-looked veterans of the war-time tugboat fleets.

On to the iron: The independent operators often look to the ocean ports for "good buys" on harbor tugs to convert for Lakes use. Capt. Hoey made this process famous with his one-after-the-other purchase of countless harbor tugs which he has hauled home through the Erie Canal or up the Mississippi towards Chicago. One particular type of tug that seems to have proven itself for Gaelic is the 1949 to 1952-vintage 88-foot welded steel hulls built by the Alexander Shipyard at New Orleans. They were generally built with 12-567A EMD engines and LST gearboxes. Upon arrival at the Gaelic yard in Detroit, the tugs were torn down to the bear bones. The tugs that were built to ABS specs had reached the point of needing an overhaul and an overhaul is just that what they got! Watching one go under the knife at Gaelic, one would think they were being scrapped rather than repaired. The company spared no expense reconstructing the tugs from the keel up including all new cabins, tight, new aluminum doors, all new machinery including main engines with typically 150% more horsepower. Finally as the shell comes together, modern electronics and all the required safety equipment gets installed as the tug receives the recognizable Gaelic paint scheme. These beautifully rebuilt "imports" make up the bulk of the Gaelic fleet today.

Zenith Tug operates one fine example of a type of tugboat that we'll touch on briefly. The seventy year-old tug *Seneca* was charted from Billington Contract-

ing in 2001, Zenith's first year in operation. Credit can be given to this tug and its owner for putting the company in business.

She carries with her a fascinating history. The *Seneca* began life in 1939 at Gulfport Boiler in Port Arthur, Texas, designed and built as a ship-docking tug for the Card Towing Company. It is also interesting to note that the Card Towing's color scheme was a dark green hull with a gold stripe and similar topside colors as well, coincidently nearly-identical to Zenith's scheme. The tug, along with the Alexander hulls Gaelic is using, was built and outfitted for service around ocean ports. Typically their aft tow-bitts are positioned too far back. For ship-towing on the Lakes off a short stern line, you need your bitts more to the middle of the tug to allow for better control of the tow. Towing off these ocean bitts can make the tug very squirrelly on a towline, hard to control, increasing the chance of getting tripped. On the Lakes, when towing in tight quarters with a very short stern towline, the line is running up to the ship at a steep angle. The tension on that line is intense at times with the tug's incredible torque and it, alone, will raise the center of gravity of the tug, creating a potentially dangerous situation.

Gaelic normally cuts the aft portion of the cabin off, usually containing crew quarters or a galley. They move the aft bulkhead forward and take the tow-bitts with them. That additional ten feet makes

The sleek looking *Susan Hoey* is captured during lay-up in this January 20, 2001, image at Gaelic's Detroit yard. The tug is an Alexander hull, rebuilt by Gaelic in 1982 after they purchased it from the Dravo Corporation. The tug had already seen service on the Great Lakes, having bounced around between many owners since its construction in 1950. It was American Tug's *Minn*, working in the Detroit area throughout the 1970s. After working from Cleveland and Toledo as Gaelic's *Newcastle*, the tug spent the better part of the 1990s in Chicago as Holly Marine's *Laura Lynn*. It was repurchased by Gaelic in 1999 and stationed at Toledo. In October 2006, the tug was sold to Zenith Tug who has placed it in service at Duluth under the name *Anna Marie Altman*. The tug was built with a canal-style low pilothouse but received a temporary upper pilothouse from time to time when not working the canal.

a huge difference. Also, the captain's quarters are normally cut off and the smoke stacks streamlined. These modifications greatly improve aft visibility for the captain not only trying to see the ship he is towing but also his crew on deck hooking up the gear.

Getting back to the *Seneca* for a little bit: The redevelopment of the harbor tug was in full swing in the 1930s as ships were getting bigger and a World War was approaching. General Motors was pushing the idea of diesel-electric tugs. The systems were nearly identical to their locomotives, but rather than a handful of traction motors, there would be one or two large propulsion motors turning a shaft through a gearbox. They contracted Gulfport, on speculation, to produce a 100-foot, 1000-SHP harbor tug. Many were completed in the late 1930s but their practicality was established during the war. The *Seneca*, which was launched as the *General*, had a few nearly-identical sisters. They include: the *Hercules*, *Vulcan*, and the *E. M. Black*, all of which lived-on after repowering to higher-horsepower diesel mains. The *General* still has her original woodwork, electric propulsion

system, 12-567A main engine, original deckhouse and all-around appearance minus her lifeboat. She is unarguably one of the prettiest tugs on the Lakes today.

Requisitioned for the war, the *General* (as *USS Keshena YN-37*) served as a net layer for positioning anti-submarine nets at harbor entrances, such as Guantanamo Bay, Cuba, where the tug was stationed through the duration of the war. As the war progressed, purpose-built net layers were far handier at laying the nets but other boats were also needed to open and close the nets to allow ships to pass. For this purpose, in 1942 the *Keshena* was redesignated YNT-5 (Yard Tug, Net Tending). She was later redesignated YTM (Yard Tug, Medium) and upon decommissioning, the tug returned to the ship-docking service, this time for McAllister Towing & Transportation at Newport News.

The *Seneca* is like so many others featured in this chapter, which have spent most of their lives on the salt water and certainly paid their dues in terms of wear and tear. Their compassionate owners on the

Still in Gaelic colors, the *Blackie B.* is laying in Burns Harbor in this December 28, 1995 image. This tug, the former *Susan Hoey*, along with their *Gaelic Challenge* (visible astern of this one) were sold to Eagle Marine Towing, a short-lived firm, who attempted to offer towing in the Chicago and Burns area. Soon both tugs were unemployed and owned by Glenn Dawson of South Chicago. The boat was built by Alexander in 1952 as the *Bonita*. In 1997 it left Chicago after being bought back by Gaelic Tug. The name *Mary Kay* was spray-painted on the hull for the trip back. Gaelic brought it back up to their standards and within a year it was resold. Today it is in service for Shepard Marine Construction and named *Robin Lynn*.

The first *Patricia Hoey* is pictured at Toledo on February 20, 1990, moored alongside the G-tug *Montana*. The tug was just purchased from Gaelic Tug and would continue to work in Toledo through 1998, when it was retired to Cleveland. Under the GLT name *New Hampshire*, it was sold off-Lakes with sister tug *Oregon* (ex-Gaelic Tug *Galway Bay*) and City-Class tug *Alaska*. After wintering in Oswego at the end of the 1998 season, the trio left the Lakes in the spring of 2000 bound for points south. Under the new names *Grouper* (ex-*Alaska*), *Gull* (ex-*Oregon*) and *Sea Tractor* (ex-*New Hampshire*), the three did not stay together long. As noted in previous captions, the *Grouper* stayed in the Erie Canal and the *Gull* was abandoned off Norfolk. However, the *Sea Tractor* made it to Florida and after an extensive rebuild, it was ready for action once again, under the name *Shark*. However, it has yet to turn a wheel commercially and has remained in lay-up at Fort Lauderdale. *Al Hart photo*

Lakes end up pouring many thousands of dollars into these old bombers to keep them going. However, after an extensive keel-up rebuild, these aging tugs are just as good as any of the newer boats on the market. They normally lack the fancy accommodations, galley and wheelhouse technology, but on the Lakes these tugs never stray far from their owner's pier. They'll run out, dock a ship or break some ice for the day or night and then head back in, getting to go home for a while until the next call.

The Alexander hulls, discussed all throughout this chapter, are another fine example of a salt-water, heavily-built, ABS inspected tugboat that have found their way into the Lakes for conversion to harbor tugs. The independent operators do not have the large fleet of custom-made tugs from the turn-of-the-century like their big corporate competitor. They make do with what they've got, reconstructing old hulls into modernly-rigged, high-horsepower capable tugs designed in-house and often specifically for the local trade they serve in. Tugs of all walks of life can be found on the Lakes with the ship-docking firms. These tugs have been brought in from other waterway territories all over the country.

The major difference between Lake ports and Ocean ports is the volume. Tugs are rarely called out on the Lakes. They only call us in desperate situations when they have break-downs or weather conditions are severe and they need tugs to hold them up against the wind while they try to enter a slip.

Operating costs are about the same. For a simplified example: let us say it costs any one tugboat company $1,000 per week to stay in business. If a steamship only needs them once a week, the rate will be $1,000. If they need the tugs five times a week, the rate for each tow would be $200. Make sense? So yes, tug rates are extremely high on the Lakes and the equipment is ancient. But remember, these companies all have to comply with the ever-increasing set of towing vessel regulations and each week hope there is work to cover their costs of waiting loyally for a ship that may need them. We provide a very unique service and as long as there is commercial navigation on the Lakes, a fleet of harbor tugs will be needed to assist. The best thing the steamship companies can do to see the rates lessen is to use the tugboats more often. The more we get used, the more flexibility we have in the rates.

For the ship owners and agents off the lakes, contracts for service are normally unheard of and towage is always negotiable. Calumet River Fleeting, Gravel & Lake, Great Lakes Towing, Gaelic Tugboat, Le Groupe Ocean, MacDonald Marine, McKeil Marine, Nadro Marine, Selvick Marine Towing, Thunder Bay Tug, and Zenith Tug all provide a respectable service with powerful tugs and well-experienced crews. Personally, as an owner and tug operator, I have great respect for each and every company named above. Each of these firms, on a daily basis, plays a vital roll in the ongoing commercial operation of our system of fresh water Lakes.

Still in GLT colors, the tug *Gull* lays more or less abandoned, at the Pungo Ferry Marina dock near Chesapeake, VA. "Transients welcome" the sign reads. I'm not sure a 90-foot harbor tug is what they meant, especially when it's towed in during the night and two years later, it's still there! The tug was GLT's second *Oregon*, acquired in the same fashion as the *Patricia Hoey* and *Wicklow*, from a partial buy-out of Gaelic Tug in 1990. The tug was built in 1952 as the *Jennifer George* and was one of many Alexander hulls bought by Gaelic Tug and rebuilt for Great Lakes service. And check out the sign once more... diesel fuel $1.15 a gallon... ahhh, the good ol' days... and that was only three years ago! The tug has since laid in the small boat harbor at Newport News and its days are likely numbered.

It's December 1998 and the tugs *Sea Tractor* and *Gull* are laying at Oswego. Outboard and not visible in the photo is the *Grouper*. The tugs are stuck for winter after having arrived a day late to beat the closing of the canal. They are still wearing the GLT colors but have their names blanked out. The *Gull*, the one that was running, had her name spray-painted on for the trip. Over winter, pipes froze and she nearly sank. The Coast Guard pumped it out and leaks were temporarily patched. The *Sea Tractor* was built in 1951 at Alexander as the *Messenger* for Suderman & Young Towing. *Jason R. LaDue Photo*

The *Gull* is powered by an 1800-HP 16-278A Cleveland diesel. Flying Gaelic's flag, the tug was based in Toledo under the name *Galway Bay* throughout the 1980s. The engine is a V-16 General Motors product. Each separate head is clearly visible on top with an elbow leading up to the exhaust manifold. On each one is a pyrometer for checking exhaust temps. The front end holds the throttle control, fuel and water pumps and the governor is towards the top. Down the sides are inspection holes with removable covers. The larger ones toward the bottom are for the crankcase, the center handholes lead to the air-box and the upper holes, just under the heads, open to the injector control shaft. Blocking the view of the center handholes is a three-piece piping manifold. Each line serves a separate function, such as fuel supply, fuel bleeding, and an over-speed trip. Hanging low on the engine's side is the always-present coffee can with a drain line from the air-box to catch the blow-by oil.

The former North American Towing tug *Wabash* now sails as the *William Hoey*. She was built for Great Lakes Dredge & Dock in 1924 as the *Martha C.* In this photo the tug is moored alongside the *Seneca*, another ex-Noramtow tug. GLD & D had some of the first big diesel tugs on the Lakes. The *Martha* was originally powered by a 6-cylinder Fairbanks Morse diesel. It was repowered in 1948 with a 12-278A Cleveland, the engine she still has today. *Al Hart photo*

In 1952 the *Martha* was renamed *Langdon C. Hardwicke*, a name she would wear for the next thirty years. North American bought the tug in 1982 and ran her to the end as the *Wabash*. Holly Marine Towing bought all the North American tugs when the company went under and they ended up keeping this one, renaming it *Katie Ann*. Gaelic bought the tug in 1999 and brought her to Detroit. Now named *William Hoey*, she is normally stationed at Toledo.

The classy *Triton* spent the first 90 years of her life working from Philadelphia. The 85-footer was built there by Neafie & Levy in 1889. In 1913 it was purchased by the Independent Pier Company owned by the Meyle family, hence the big 'M' on her stack. In 1980, Independent was bought-out by McAllister Towing and the beautifully maintained Meyle tugs were replaced in short order with those of greater horsepower. A year later the *Triton, Trojan,* and McAllister's own *Mary L. McAllister* were sold to the newly formed North American Towing Company based in Chicago. *Dave Boone collection*

Decades later, the *Triton* heads up a row of retired tugboats in Lemont, IL at Egan's yard. Now named *Robin E.*, she is among friends, lying alongside her former Philly fleetmate *Denise E.* (ex-*Trojan*, 1912), the famous Dunbar & Sullivan tug *Derek E.* (ex-*Sachem*, 1907), and finally the *Becky E.* (ex-*DPC-51*, 1943). The tugs are all EMD powered but have been mothballed for over a decade in this July 2006 image. North American Towing shut down in 1991 and the Egan family purchased the bulk of their fleet through Holly Marine. The former *Trojan* came to the Meyle fleet, purchased "as is, where is" from P. F. Martin in 1948 after a sinking on the Schuylkill River.

The *Robin E.* is powered by a 12-cylinder EMD 567C with a Falk LST gearbox. This is a common arrangement on harbor tugs powered in the 1940s and 50s. The combinations of 12-cylinder A-model EMDs and horizontal offset Falk gearboxes were mostly WW-II surplus sets built for or removed from LST landing crafts. The one on the old *Triton* appears to be in very nice shape, with the exception of her air-box and crankcase inspection-hole covers open and a few jumper lines scavenged. On the back end of the engine her gearbox and clutch can be seen. In front of the engine, part of a fuel tank is visible. These large round fuel tanks on her and the *Trojan* are valuable in the eyes of prospective buyers. Most old tugs had fuel tanks integral with the hull, increasing the risk of a spill, should the hull plate be punctured.

In Norfolk, August 14, 1975, the *Mary L. McAllister* is backing down, holding her position while awaiting a ship. The 1939-built harbor tug is now working on the Great Lakes in Duluth as the *Seneca*. It was built by Gulfport Boiler Works as their Hull No. 131. Throughout the years, many salt-water tugs have found their way into the hands of Great Lakes operators. This tug has always had a strong spray of cooling water discharge. Choking it down can often reduce loss of suction. Backing down will cause cavitation against the hull and the system can become air-bound. *George R. Schneider photo*

Today the old *Mary L. McAllister* looks about the same as she did in her days docking ships around Norfolk. Aside from a different paint scheme and some heavy ice breaking, the *Seneca* is still serving the purpose she was built for nearly seventy years ago. The transition to fresh water saved this tug's life. Plenty more just like her and better have gone to the scrappers or intentionally scuttled on the reefs. On the Lakes, however, the old single screw tugs function quite well. The tug was built for the Card Towing Company as the *General* but was renamed *Raymond Card* after just a few months. Then in 1940 it was requisitioned by the U.S. Navy for service as a submarine net-tender in Guantanamo Bay, Cuba. The tug was rechristened *USS Keshena YTM-731*. The tug was later decommissioned and sold to McAllister Towing. As an ironic side note, another tug named *USS Keshena* was called in to assist a stranded ship out of a minefield. While doing so, the tug hit one, blew her hull open, and now rests on the bottom of the Atlantic off North Carolina. It has been misidentified in Navy publications as the 1939 *Keshena*. The true sunken *Keshena* was actually a 150-foot Shipping Board tug built in 1919 by Whitney Brothers in Superior, the very place the surviving *Keshena* is working today!

It's January 15, 2005, and the *Seneca* is busy helping the steamer *Arthur M. Anderson* into her lay-up berth for winter. Another AAA-class steamer, Oglebay Norton's *Reserve*, had just come in and is moored behind her. Ice conditions can get ugly on the Lakes, especially in the Twin Ports of Duluth, MN and Superior, WI. Tugs are put to the test, often having to back and ram their way through heavy ice come spring fit-out. The ships ran late into the winter this year and after the last ore boats came in, the *Seneca* was the last vessel to lay-up after the 2004 season, working until January 22, 2005.

Flows of broken harbor ice can pack tightly in the slips. The tugs will run in prior to a ship's arrival and bust out the slip, loosening the ice and doing their best to flush it out of the slip. Additional areas of the harbor or slip heads must be broken out as well, in order to give the ice a place to go when the massive ship slides into her berth, pushing a tremendous pile of ice from its way. Here, the tug *Seneca* has broken out the C. Reiss aggregate dock up the St. Louis River and the captain has her nosed up against a steamship, pinning it to the dock while crews get her cables out. The date is December 24, 2004, and there are 26 crewmembers aboard that old ship and three more on the tug spending another holiday away from their families.

Mid-March is fit-out time for the ships on the Great Lakes. At Duluth, the *John J. Boland* and *Roger Blough* are laid up in the Garfield C — Port Terminal slip. It's March 22nd and the *Seneca* is breaking the *Blough* loose for another season of carrying taconite from Two Harbors to the lower Lakes. The *Seneca* is a diesel electric tug powered by her original machinery. The main engine in this 1939-vintage harbor tug is a 12-cylinder EMD 567A diesel. The electric tugs are very smooth to operate since you can apply the power gently and turn the propulsion motor very slowly. Also, the relatively long shafts and gearboxes of a clutch boat are easier to damage if the wheel hits heavy ice. Captains are careful to back only in their tracks, never into solid ice.

Selvick's *Carla Ann Selvick* and *Jacquelyn Nicole* are stationed at Green Bay in this June 2004 photo. The former G-tug was North American Towing's *Dakota*, stationed at Duluth. The *Carla Ann* was built in Baltimore in 1908 as the *S. O. Co. No. 19,* for the Standard Oil Company. It was purchased by McAllister Towing in 1953 and became the *Roderick McAllister* a few years later. Arthur Fournier bought the tug in 1981 and worked it out of Bath, ME, docking ships at Bath Iron Works. In 1984 the tug was purchased by Selvick and brought to the Great Lakes through the Erie Canal. Originally it had a Skinner fore and aft compound steam engine, 17-1/2-inch and 33-inch cylinder bore and a 26-inch stroke. That was replaced in 1943 with a 12-567A EMD. Not long after Selvick bought the tug, her engine went down and a 12-567C was reinstalled. If you look closely, you will notice that her top deck is all still the original wood construction, quite rare these days!

The cabin and pilothouse off Gaelic's *Galway* rest at Kewaunee in January 1985 after the tug was cut up for scrap late the previous year. The tug was purchased by Selvick Marine Towing in 1982 as two-for-one deal with the *G. F. Becker* (now Selvick's *Baldy B.*). The *Galway* was engineless and served no purpose so was cut up for scrap and her pilothouse saved. If you compare this pilothouse with the one on the *Carla Ann Selvick* in the previous photo, you will notice they are the same. To get through the Erie Canal, the top of the *Carla's* wooden pilothouse had to be cut off with a chainsaw and a new temporary plywood roof made. This was all removed upon arrival in Kewaunee and over the winter of 1984-85, the old pilothouse off the canaller *Galway* was reinstalled on the *Carla*. *Wendell Wilke photo*

Not a true "G-tug," the *North Carolina* is pictured at the Duluth Port Terminal dock in this cold December 28, 1996, image. The tug has been breaking ice for the steamer *Lee A. Tregurtha* and is now standing by behind her stern. The tug was acquired by the Towing Company in a partial buy-out of Gaelic Tug in the early 1990s. It had operated as Gaelic's *Wicklow* in Cleveland but before that was U.S. Steel's *Limestone*, based at Rogers City. Gaelic bought it in 1982 and towed it home to Detroit (the tug had not run in a few years). It just happens to be powered by a 12-cylinder Cleveland 278A with a diesel-electric propulsion system, like many G-tugs.

Another imitation G-tug, acquired through a 1990 buy-out, is the *Missouri*, based at the Soo. This tug began life as the steamer *Rogers City*. She was built in 1927 by American Shipbuilding's Lorain yard. The U.S. Steel company, Michigan Limestone, was her initial owner. Its name was changed in 1956 to *Dolomite* but U.S. Steel maintained ownership until 1981 when the tug was sold to John Wellington at the Sault Ste. Marie-based Seaway Towing Company. Capt. Wellington reconstructed the tug, removing its 800-IHP steam engine and in its place, put a 2250-HP Alco 12-251F diesel. The tug was renamed *Chippewa* and went into service at the Soo. It is pictured below the Soo Locks on May 13, 2005, waiting for an upbound ocean-going freighter, which it will assist through the locks.

The big lake tug *Georgia* is the second tug to bear that name for the Towing Company. The first was a standard Type 2 G-tug built in 1916 but scrapped at Ashtabula in 1966. This second *Georgia* was built for the Corps of Engineers in 1895 by John Dialogue & Son at Camden, NJ. The 108-foot tug was launched as the *Lamont*. Roen Salvage brought her into the Lakes in 1935, renaming it *John Roen*. Great Lakes Towing subsidiary Petco (Clark Towing) purchased the tug in 1950 and a few years later it was transferred to the Towing Company and named *Samuel E. Bool*. At that time she was repowered to diesel with a 12-567A. The engine was changed again in 1967, this time to a C-block. She was given her state name in 1972. The tug had been reconstructed during her repowering, adding modern doors and an aluminum pilothouse. The *Georgia* was cut up for scrap in 1998, not far from the GLT headquarters in Cleveland.

In June of 2000, McKeil Marine of Hamilton purchased two big ship-docking tugs, the *Carrol C. I* and the *Bonnie B. III*. Here, the *Bonnie* is working as the stern tug on a ship-assist. The line off her bow is leading up to the ship's stern. Originally the tug was the U.S. Flag *San Nicholas I*, built at Gulfport Shipbuilding in 1969. *Author's collection*

Something missing? Her pilothouse! Gravel & Lake Service's tug *Robert John* is in lay-up at Thunder Bay, undergoing a rebuild in November of 1998. The tug was built by Canadian Dredge & Dock in 1945 for the Royal Canadian Navy's Glenn-Class as the *Gleneagle*. It was purchased by the famous Foundation Maritime in 1947 and renamed *Bansturdy*. Her Vivian diesel was replaced in 1973 with a 1200-HP 12-567C EMD engine. Gravel & Lake purchased the boat in 1966 and provided her present name.

In 1998 the old pilothouse of the *Robert John* was chopped off. After wintering like that, the tug actually spent another year wheelhouseless, for lack of a better term, before crews constructed a new one. This unusual view is from the top of the front steps, looking down into the galley through a big hole where her pilothouse once sat. Today the tug is back in action with a beautiful new modern pilothouse.

The classic harbor tug *Glenlea* was built by Russel Brothers at Owen Sound in 1943 for the Royal Canadian Navy. Originally the 82-footer had an 8-cylinder 360-HP slow-speed Vivian diesel engine. Like her sister *Robert John*, the tug was purchased by Foundation in 1947. At that time she was renamed *Bansaga*. In 1964 the tug was brought to Lake Superior upon purchase by Gravel & Lake Services. They repowered the tug with a 12-567C EMD and gave it her present name of *George N. Carleton*. The proud looking tug, wooden pilothouse and all, is posed at Thunder Bay ready for her next job.

At Thunder Bay, the *Point Valour* and *Glenada* have just fired their engines in preparation for a ship-docking job on this calm night in November 1998. The *Glenada* was built by Russel Brothers in 1944 for the Canadian Navy. Thunder Bay Tug Services bought her in 1995. Not long before this photo was taken, the *Glenada* and her crew were credited with saving the lives of those aboard the shipwrecked passenger vessel *Grandpa Woo II*, which had been ripped from its moorings and was powerless in Force 11 winds on Lake Superior. The violent storm was about the worst anyone had seen from both vessels. After 10 hours adrift, the *Glenada* located the wreck and was able to safely get her crew aboard the tug before the violent seas beat the helpless ship against the rocks until it finally broke up and sank. Today the tug is hard at work in the busy grain port of Thunder Bay on the top end of Lake Superior.

The *Glenada* is a beautiful tug all-around with a spotless interior. Here, you see her woodwork, stainless and brass gleam, showing the pride of her crew. A large wooden binnacle stands in the front center, holding the ship's compass. The photo shows she is well fit, with every navigational aid and monitoring device imaginable. The *Glenada* is powered by a single 1100-HP Caterpillar D399 diesel which had replaced a Vivian engine in 1977.

Laid up behind the steamer *Willowglen* sits the former Canadian McAllister tug *Cathy McAllister*. She is officially named *Seven Sisters* in this March 2003 photo, although the name is nowhere to be found on the hull. She was built in 1954 by Davie Shipbuilding. She worked for Canada Steamship Lines at Quebec City under the name *Charlie S.* until being sold to McAllister in 1975. Donal G. McAllister, a fourth-generation member in the family tugboat business and president of the company, named the tug after his daughter Cathy. The tug was sold surplus in 2002. On November 2nd of that year, the tug was under tow of the *Salvage Monarch* bound for Goderich when, in a heavy storm and snow squall, the towline parted and the *Seven Sisters* was set adrift with no lights. The Canadian Coast Guard cutter *Griffon* located the lone tug the following day and the tow was put back together.

It's about time for spring fit-out and if there is one port left on the continent that proves beyond doubt you do *not* need 6000-HP Z-drive tugs to dock a ship, it's the Port of Goderich, Ontario. Here a handful of small 45-footers handle the job quite well, turning the ships and assisting them in and out of port. MacDonald Marine operates a fleet of four tugs in the Goderich Harbour. At the stern of the *Ian Mac*, its operator is working a big pry bar to bust open the ice around her stern. Must break out the tugs first before they can go break out the ships!

The old junker *Glenmont* rests near the Toronto Dry Dock in this January 1998 photo. She was one of many wartime Russel tugs built for the Royal Canadian Navy. Still wearing her original name, the 82-foot tug has been privately owned since the 1980s and her condition in this photo should be a lesson to many; if a tug is not making you money, get rid of it! They are costly to maintain and keep up to today's ever-increasing inspection standards. In 2000 the tug was pulled up and, oddly enough, converted to a yacht. Her cabin was stripped and a new one built on top of the new framing and hull plating that was added, giving her extra length and breadth. You could probably hold in one hand the amount of 1943 steel left in her today.

McKeil Marine's *Glenbrook* was built in 1944 by Russel Brothers at Owen Sound for the Royal Canadian Navy, another of the Glen-Class. The tug was powered by a 400-HP Enterprise diesel. McKeil purchased the tug in 1979 and within a year converted the tug to triple screw. The mains consist of a center Detroit 8V-92 and two 8V-71 wing engines. The tug was sold in the late 1990s and went to Trinidad. *Author's collection*

The *Lac Como* is busy flushing ice for a saltie about to exit a lock in the Welland Canal on December 20, 1994. Canadian Bridge built the tug in 1944 for the Canadian Government. The 65-footer was sold to McKeil in 1966 along with sister tugs *Lac Erie*, *Lac Manitoba*, and *Lac Vancouver*. All four tugs were powered by 8-cylinder Vivian engines. *Jimmy Sprunt photo*

Nadro Marine's *Progress* was built by Russel Brothers in 1948 as the *P. J. Murer* for Canadian International Paper. The boat was renamed *Michael D. Misner* in 1981 for Great Lakes Contractors. In 1993 she became the first vessel in the Lower Lakes Towing fleet. Interestingly, from their early beginnings with that one lone tug, they have now become one of the more prominent fleets on the Lakes, operating twelve freighters. The 80-foot tug was powered by a DMG-38 Enterprise which was removed in 2000 at Nadro's Port Dover yard. Advertised for sale, the engine was purchased by a tour boat company for parts. Their vessel had twin DMG-38s and the engine from the tug was found to be too good to use just for parts and it actually replaced one of the engines in the passenger ship. The *Progress* was then converted to twin screw and a pair of 1000-HP Detroit 12V-149TI diesels added. *Capt. Gerry Ouderkirk photo*

McKeil Marine's *Jarrett McKeil* was built by Davie Shipbuilding in 1956 for the yard's own use. After twenty years of service, the boat was sold to Quebec Tugs and continued to serve the Seaway and eastern Great Lakes. The tug is still powered by her original 1200-HP 12-278A Cleveland diesel. Later in life a towing machine was added to her stern. Also, her pilothouse windows have been replaced with something a little more modern, as have the doors on her main deckhouse. Originally named *Robert B. No. 1*, the tug received its current name in 1997. The tug is pictured at McKeil's Hamilton yard on March 1, 1999, moored alongside the old towboat *Manco*. Behind the pair, the *Doug McKeil* rests in dry-dock.

The Chesapeake & Ohio's big tug *A. T. Lowmaster* was built at the Newport News Shipbuilding & Drydock Company as their Hull No. 468. It and sister tug *R. J. Bowman* (Hull No. 467) were patterned after the 1937 *F. M. Whitaker*, also a Newport hull. The keels were laid down in October of 1947. The *Lowmaster* was launched on February 24, 1948, and completed and delivered to the C&O Railway a couple months later. It entered service moving coal barges in the Chesapeake Bay area. The 110-foot tug was equipped with scotch boilers also built by Newport News Shipbuilding. The main was an impressive 1000-IHP fore and aft compound reciprocating steam engine. Railroad tugs mostly hipped their barges, which is evident by her well-fendered sides. The tug was eventually sold into Canadian registry and brought into the Lakes as the *Wilfred M. Cohen. Author's collection*

Chapter 3
Harbor Tugs: General Towing

Not small tugs, not large tugs, not really ship-docking tugs… what shall we call these old girls? In any commercial harbor a number of tugs can be found engaged in odd jobs, whether it be a niche market or a combination of tasks as described in other chapters of this book. The same tug that may be handling a lake-tow might be found docking a ship the next day or moving barges within the port.

Contractors, in addition to owning large lake tugs and small tenders, often operate medium size tugs used for hauling heavy scows laden with dredge spoils to the off-loading site after having been dug from the harbor's bottom. Throughout history railroads have owned large tugboats built with tall superstructures for moving railcar ferries across rivers and harbors. Fleeting and shifting companies use a wide range of different style tugs for moving barges around the river systems and delivering them to their appropriate destination in or near the port of arrival.

Other tugs that could certainly qualify as ship-docking tugs have been built with the barge trade in mind, dragging scows back and forth within the harbor or to and from close-by ports. Many of these were government-built during times of war but now are owned and operated by civilian tugboat companies. Some tugs have been built for the pulpwood trade, towing large rafts of logs normally from a small harbor or river near the logging grounds across the Lakes to the mills. This chapter will look at a wide range of these multi-duty tugboats in a wide variety of shapes and sizes. The common theme with these tugs is simply: no limits.

Today the *Wilfred M. Cohen* is a member of the Purvis fleet based at Sault Ste. Marie. In this May 24, 1992, photo, she is wearing the colors of the McLean fleet, her owner from 1981 through 1994. The tug is downbound at Mission Point pushing the lumber barge *McAllister 132*. The tug's wooden cabin has been replaced and its steam engine is long gone as well. Today the tug's main engine is a 10-cylinder 38D8-1/8 Fairbanks Morse diesel that had once powered the WW-II era submarine *USS Finback*. *Jon LaFontaine photo*

At Thunder Bay, Ontario, the former Norfolk & Western Railway's unusual tug *F. A. Johnson* has been retired for many years. It was used to push cross-river rail ferries at Detroit with its sister tug, the *R. G. Cassidy*. Upon retirement in 1994 the tug was sold to Gravel & Lake Services. Her two EMD 12-567C engines were removed in 1995 and used to repower Gaelic's big tug *Roger Stahl*. The *Johnson* was built in 1952 at Houston by the Parker Brothers Shipyard. The tug was originally named *Capt. Chas T. Parker* but after only a couple years became the *Rapid Cities*. It first served in the Gulf before coming to the Lakes in 1970.

At Philadelphia in 1940, the tug *Anna Sheridan* has a bow line on an old wooden scow as her boiler and 250-IHP steam engine put out some serious smoke. The tug was built in 1903 in Philly as the *Radiant.* In 1977 it was sold Canadian and came into the Lakes with the name *Princess No. 1.* The 80-foot harbor tug was repowered in 1952 with a 12-567A EMD engine. *Photo courtesy of Dave Boone*

The *Princess No. 1* was already named *Princess* when Wakeham & Sons brought her into Canadian registry. The *No. 1* was added to distinguish the tug from another already of that name. In this August 18, 2001, photo at Windsor, the tug is mothballed along with the former City-Class G-tug *Jenny T. II* (*Ashtabula*, 1915). Both tugs were owned by the Gayton family and laid up due to lack of work. The *Princess* is now laid up on the Rouge River in Detroit. At 106-years old and in need of repair, her future is uncertain.

Not original but still "classic." The pilothouse of the *Princess No. 1* shows the signs of her 1952 repowering. A massive steering wheel is typical of the Sperry systems found on many tugboats. On the throttle stand to the right is an extension-cord wired electric joystick for steering. This "mobile" unit allows the captain to go outside when steering for better visibility. In some cases, they've even been known to climb up on the roof with the control run out a window, while a deckhand watches the throttle. An engine tachometer is above the door, and in the center a spotlight control handle is protruding from the ceiling. The rope for the horn runs across the ceiling and then, oddly, through two pulleys, straight down to the floor. I guess if the captain ends up passed out on the floor, at least he can still blow the whistle. Ahhh, the good ol' days.

The Corps of Engineers tug *Essayons* was built in 1908 by the Racine-Truscott-Shell Lake Boat Company at Muskegon. The Corps owned it through 1950 when it was acquired by the Marine Iron shipyard in Duluth. The tug was refit and sold to the Zenith Dredge Company, who, in addition to a contracting firm, also operated a shipyard in the port. The two yards, Marine Iron and Zenith Dredge, built all of the 180-foot Coast Guard buoy tenders during WW-II. The *Essayons* is captured here at night with the old Superwood plant in the background of the Duluth Timber dock. Both properties were once used by the Zenith Dredge Company; this was their home slip.

The *Essayons* was retired in the 1960s with their big steam tug *William A. Whitney*. The pair sat out of service side by side until the *Whitney* was finally sold to Gaelic Tug. Zenith had hopes of repowering the *Essayons* but it was never needed and finally just before the firm went out of business, the tug was sold to a private party. Its big steam engine had already been removed in the 1970s and was one of the original exhibits in the marine museum at Duluth's Canal Park. In 1993, the tug's boiler was removed and the tug was gutted for conversion to a live-aboard. Over time the old steamer had many structural modifications such as repositioning of her ventilators, hull portholes plated over, wooden rub-rails and rail cap removed, and a towing machine added. In addition, her pilothouse was raised a bit and square windows replaced portholes. Captain's quarters were also constructed, behind the pilothouse. In this image, Zenith has removed her steam engine (pictured on the dock in front of the crane) in preparation for a transplant at the marine museum. *Author's collection*

The ancient *William A. Whitney* can still be found afloat in South Chicago in the Hannah reserve fleet. Painted flat black for the movie *Road to Perdition,* it was used in the filming but her scenes were cut from the final edit. The 112-footer was built of riveted steel from leftover WW-I contracts at the Whitney Brothers yard in Superior. They used it for general towing and barge duties near the Twin Ports. The tug was later sold to Merritt, Chapman & Scott (a large contractor) and in 1963 back to the Duluth area for the Zenith Dredge Company. It went into lay-up in the late 1960s and sat around with fleetmate *Essayons* in hopes for a repowering but that day never came. In 1975, Gaelic's tug *Donegal* arrived to haul the old *Whitney* to its new home in Detroit. Gaelic repowered the vessel with a 10-cylinder opposed piston Fairbanks Morse engine out of the Coast Guard cutter *Eastwind.*

The galley of the *William A. Whitney* is a submarine galley, meaning below the main deck. In this case, it is behind the engine room above the shaft. In this image, the curve of the stern is very apparent and against the walls are "built in" refrigeration cabinets with thick insulated wooden doors. If you open those, the back wall of the "fridge" is riveted hull plate. The natural cooling of the cold lake water against the hull works well in this case. Under your feet, while sitting down to eat, are floor plates that open up right to the spinning shaft.

It wouldn't be a tugboat book without including the famous *Edna G.,* the former railroad tug that proudly served Two Harbors, MN its entire life. Today the tug is practically the City's mascot. It was built in 1896 at Cleveland Shipbuilding for the Duluth & Iron Range Railway for service in Two Harbors, a port she only left briefly during WW-I. The tug was the last steam-fired tugboat in regular commercial service on the Great Lakes when it was retired in 1981.

The stern section of the *Ruth Hindman* rests half sunk off Bayfield, Ontario in this December 2004 image. The 120-foot tug was built over the winter of 1908-09 at Lorain by American Shipbuilding. It was ordered new by the Duluth, Missabe & Northern Railway for use at its West Duluth ore docks. The big fire tug was originally named *William A. McGonagle*, in honor of the Railway's president and general manager. Upon arrival at Duluth on May 10, 1909, headlines read, "Greatest Fire Tug in the World Reaches Duluth." She was powered by a 2-cylinder steam engine with two turbine-driven centrifugal fire pumps which could move 12,000-gallons of water per minute at 150-PSI. The tug was sold Canadian in 1935 and worked in the pulpwood trade until 1966 when it was sold to Siddal Fisheries for conversion to a fishing vessel. This conversion never took place and on a scrap tow the vessel was lost. Today, this is all that remains of the fire fighter that was once the pride of Duluth.

Abandoned in very shallow water near Gypsum in Sandusky Bay, the former steam tug *J. P. Manning* faces the shoreline wearing a sad expression. The old tug was built in 1906 by Johnston Brothers at Ferrysburg, MI. The 70-foot harbor tug was first owned by the Lake Shore & Michigan Southern Railroad at Cleveland. In 1921 the tug was transferred to the New York Central Railroad at Ashtabula. The boat was sold to a contractor in 1927 and renamed *B. E. West*, a name she carried right to the end. Merritt, Chapman & Scott bought the *West* in 1951 and the corporation's name is still clearly visible on her bow.

The old wooden green hull of the *Edward E. Gillen* can still be seen at Milwaukee where she was stripped and abandoned in the 1950s. The 75-foot tug was built in 1928 at Sturgeon Bay Shipbuilding for Gillen, the tug's one-owner. Its steel over-plating is starting to separate itself from the hull as the old tug rots away. Abandonments such as this were once a common sight in nearly every harbor. As natural deterioration and waterfront beautification projects swept through our ports, they have all but disappeared. A modern tug owned by Gillen bearing the same name can be found further on in this chapter.

The cobbled up riveted hull of the 1928 *Bonnie G. Selvick* shows its eighty years of hard miles in this August 2001 image at Superior. The tug was built by Manitowoc Shipbuilding for the Fitzsimons & Connell Dredge & Dock Company. The tug was later owned by Merritt-Chapman & Scott and Dunbar & Sullivan before being sold to Selvick in 1977. At that time her original name of *E. James Fucik* was scrubbed and the boat renamed honoring owner William Selvick's wife. The old low-profile tug was sold to TNT Dredging in late 2000. It left the Lakes in 2005, bound for Luka, MS on the Tenn-Tom with a hydraulic dredge and tug *Joyce Marie*. During her TNT days, the *Selvick* name was painted over on her nameboards and the tug referred to simply as the *Bonnie G*. However, the full name was kept on her documentation.

The low-profile tug *Chicago Harbor No. 4* is pictured here at — you guessed it — Chicago. The old riveted tug was built in 1903 by Johnston Brothers in Ferrysburg. Its original name was *Bonita*, meaning "pretty" in Portuguese. I'm not sure if that's where the name came from for this particular tug, but the translation fits. The sleek old harbor tug resembles that of the classic G-tug. Barnaby purchased the tug in 1957 from the City of Chicago. The old tug sat unused for a while, but eventually he renamed it *Eddie B.* and put it in service moving barges in the Chicago area until its sale into the contracting trade as the *Ludington*, where it served for Bultema, Canonie, and most recently the King Company. During its contracting career, the vessel was rebuilt to a more modern arrangement, including a retractable pilothouse. Today the tug is Andrie's *Ronald J. Dahlke. Author's collection*

Abandoned at Jacksonville, Gaelic's old *Kinsale* has her nose in the bank and her stern sunk on the Trout Creek in this February 24, 2003, photo. The tug began life as the *J. Raymond Russell*. The Russell-class included some of the most beautiful tugs ever built. They were built by the Liberty Dry Dock Company at Brooklyn in the late 1930s. The graceful lines and classy interior woodwork made these tugs true classics. Capt. Hoey purchased the tug from McAllister Towing (at that time, named *Muriel McAllister*) in 1975 and brought her into the Lakes. Originally built with a low-profile canal house, it was cut off and raised quite a bit for the barge trade. It was repowered with a 12-567C and renamed *Kinsale*. By the late 1980s the tug was getting tired and multiple breakdowns lead to her nickname *Cantsail*. It was sold to foreign interests and left the Lakes bound for Charleston in 1991. Sadly, Jacksonville seems to have been the end of the line for this proud old tug.

A few similarities exist between the *Eddie B.*, in the previous photo, and this other Barnaby tug, the *Cindy B.* Both were old riveted hulls repowered with Caterpillar 398 diesels. Both were later converted to canallers with the addition of a telescoping pilothouse. Both were purchased by Barnaby for use in Chicago and later sold into the construction trade. And finally, both were bought by the King Company in 1991. This one is currently King's *Julie Dee*, the third tug to bear that name. As the *Cindy B.*, in this April 1990 photo, she is on charter to Inland Steel and is busy shifting barges at Indiana Harbor. It is interesting to see a relatively small vessel wearing colors identical to those found on the big Inland Steel ore carriers. *Al Hart photo*

The Gillen Company at Milwaukee is known for its neat appearance. The Gulf-style twin-screw tug *Edward E. Gillen III* is only eight years old in this April 1996 photo at its home pier in Milwaukee. The tug was built at Houma, LA by Terrebonne Fabricators and is powered by a pair of KT38-M Cummins diesels. The Paterson steamer *Mapleglen* is in the background loading grain.

At the Kadinger yard in Milwaukee, the *Jake M. Kadinger* and the *David Kadinger* are tied up in this September 8, 2002, image. The *Jake* came to the Lakes in 2000 but left again in 2004 and is now in service from Florida to the Bahamas. The fairly modern looking tug was built as the *Seacor Safety* in 1984 at Escatawpa, MS as Hull No. 49. The *David* had been in the Kadinger fleet since the late 1980s, but was sold in 2005 with most all of their floating equipment. Today she is Gillen's *Jullane J.*

The tug *Jason A. Kadinger* is docked at Kadinger's Waukegan yard on September 19, 1997. Obviously not quite ready for action, the Gulf-style tug is undergoing a reconstruction after a 1994 sinking on Lake Michigan. The tug is powered by a pair of Detroit 8V-71 diesels. It was originally named *Milly Lee* and built in 1963 in Louisiana by St. Charles Steel Works. Sold when Kadinger downsized in 2005, the tug is now Gillen's *Kristin J.* and still working from the same port.

The classy looking tug *Jenny L.* has a rich history beginning in 1909 as the fish tug *Lorain*. It was built in Buffalo for the Ranney Fish Company of Cleveland. The 68-foot hull was converted to a towing vessel in 1924 and retained her 125-HP steam engine. The tug was rebuilt and renamed *Harry S. Price* in 1956. Her hull was "bustled" at that time, with new plate being welded in place over her old worn-out riveted hull. She was repowered at Toledo's Hans Hansen shipyard with a 550-HP model MD-4 Clark-Dresser large bore diesel. It was operated by the Price Brothers until 1969 when the City of Toledo purchased her for conversion to a fire tug. This conversion never took place and the tug was removed from documentation and entered lay-up. *Author's collection*

The *Harry S. Price* returned to documentation in 1973 and re-entered service as a tugboat. It was resold in the early 1980s to Trident Marine Construction. Her first job for this firm was on the construction of the Port Huron water inlet. The tug was repowered in 1984 with an 850-HP Caterpillar D398. It was named *Jenny L.* for owner Jim Collins' daughter, Jenny Lynn Collins. In 1999 the tug was sold to Lake Michigan Contractors and placed ashore at Bay Shipbuilding. The tug was never used and finally, in the spring of 2003, was given to Basic Marine Towing and taken to their Escanaba shipyard where it is pictured, minus her pilothouse and smokestack, which were removed upon arrival. As of 2006, that is as far as the project has gotten.

Luedtke's *Kurt Luedtke* is shoving the empty dump scow *No. 17* through East Gate in the Duluth harbor after having unloaded at Erie Pier. The firm had the local dredging contract in 1997. The *Kurt* was built as the *Miss Lana* in 1956 at Lockport, MS and has been in the construction trade its entire career.

Andrie's *Maribeth Andrie* is working late this season. The date is January 9, 1999, and the tug has her hands full with packed ice at Ferrysburg. The 2200-HP tug was originally named *Gladys Bea*. It was built in the Gulf in1961 but didn't get to the Lakes until the 1970s. It was the Bultema tug *American Viking* and was given her present name in 1983, during the Canonie days. The tug was sold in 2005 to the King Company and renamed *Matt Allen*. *Steve Elve photo*

The St. Lawrence Seaway Development Corporation owns and operates the well-known *Robinson Bay* from Massena, NY. The 103-foot tug was built by the Christy Corporation in 1958. The tug has a diesel-electric propulsion system which originally had a Cleveland 8-498 diesel turning its generator. In 1991, that engine was replaced with an 1800-HP Cat 3606. At the same time a 3rd level was added, providing a pilothouse with much better visibility over her barge. The tug is employed in the buoy tending service and sees the occasional ice breaking and ship assistance job as well. In this 1986 photo, the *Robbie* is seen in her original configuration. *Jimmy Sprunt photo*

On April 8, 1996, Selvick's *Susan M. Selvick* is parked in the 104th Street slip in South Chicago. The tug came down from Sturgeon Bay in the summer of 1994. It was originally the *Sanita*, built by the Liberty Drydock at Brooklyn in 1954. She was on trash scow duty in New York City for the Department of Sanitation. Ralph Eder brought the tug into the Lakes in 1977. Selvick bought the tug in 1981 with the barge *Moby Dick*. Shortly after this photo was taken the tug was renamed *Nathan S.*, in honor of the owner's son. During 1999 its pilothouse was chopped off and a new jack-up house was built for use around those Chicago bridges. Today the tug sails as the *John A. Perry* and is powered by an EMD 8-567C with 645 guts and a 3:1 Falk gear. To allow better aft visibility from the wheelhouse, the tug has had a portion of its aft cabin cut off and its stack cut down, which is apparent already in this 1996 image.

It's time for the annual Detroit River tugboat races and McQueen Marine's *Atomic* has come to join in. An old steam G-tug is doing its best to catch up. The *Atomic* was another Russel Brothers hull, built in 1945 at Owen Sound as their Hull No. 102. The 82-footer was originally powered by a big 6-cylinder DMG-36 Enterprise but in 1996, the Cat 398 from the dredge *Niagara II* was installed. However, the engine had been damaged from a sinking and failed almost immediately. The Cat came right out and a Detroit 12V-149T was put in place with the Cat gear. Over the winter of 2005-2006, Nadro Marine rebuilt the tug and installed kort nozzles. The machinery was removed but its engine was reinstalled as the port side engine in a twin-screw configuration. The tug, now powered by twin Detroit 12V-149T engines and MG-540 gears, is operated by McKeil from Hamilton. *Author's collection*

At Sarnia, March 2002, McNally's *Sandra Mary* is moored for lay-up. Behind her the lakers *Algowood* and *Peter R. Cresswell* are also snuggled in for winter. The tug was built in 1962 by Russel Brothers as Pitt's *Flo Cooper*. The orange and black colored tug was well known around the Lakes, hauling the contractor's dredges and barges from job to job. The tug was built with a V-12 EMD 567A engine. *Jason R. LaDue photo*

The *Vigilant I* is yet another 1944 Russel hull built for the Navy. She was launched as the *Glenlivet II* and powered by a 6-cylinder Enterprise. It was repowered in 1980 with a Detroit 16V-71. The tug passed through the hands of several owners, including McKeil, but was acquired by Nadro Marine in 2002. She is wearing their colors in this March 2003 photo at Port Dover. They had just completed a reconstruction of the tug, converting her to twin screw with kort nozzles and new 700-HP Detroit 16V-71TI diesels.

Nadro Marine's *Miseford* was based at Port Dover in this March 1, 1999, photo. The tug was originally steam powered but repowered in 1949 with a four-pack of Detroit 6-71 diesels through a common gearbox to a single screw. The 85-footer was built in 1915 by Matthew Beatty & Sons. Originally a huge fish tug, it was converted to a fisheries patrol vessel in 1922. Finally in 1940, the McLean family converted it to a towing tug. After a brief ownership by Purvis in the 1990s, Nadro picked up the boat in 1996 and ran her for eight years before selling it to Thunder Bay Tug Services in 2004. Today the tug is in ship-docking service at Thunder Bay on the top of Lake Superior, still sporting its original name.

Another McQueen tug, the *Patricia McQueen*, is making an appearance at the Detroit tug races. No, the fellow standing outside the pilothouse door isn't wearing a dress, he's the cook. It's pretty rare to find a cook on a harbor tug today—plenty of stale donuts though. The *Patricia* was named after J. Earl McQueen's wife, Patsy. The boat was one of several huge city-class fish tugs built for Booth Fisheries at American Shipbuilding in Lorain. This one was launched in 1911 as the *Baltimore*. It was sold Canadian in 1936 and converted to a towing vessel by McQueen Marine Ltd. At that time its steam engine was replaced by a 6-cylinder 240-HP Fairbanks Morse model 35C10 diesel. The tug has a colorful history, one probably worthy of a book on its own. Today it languishes in a Port Dover boneyard on the Canadian side of Lake Erie, going by the name *Jiggs. Author's collection*

On the blocks in the Fraser Shipyard dry-dock is the 1908 tugboat *Mount McKay*. Out of the water, the 80-foot tug really shows her size—compare to the tug's owner standing by the bow. The old riveted hull plate is overdue for some repair. In November of 2002, the tug nearly sank after being holed out in the ice. Workers spent two days trying to slow the leaks and stabilize the tug for winter lay-up. She made it through winter and in the spring after the ships left, the vulnerable old tug went into the dry-dock for replating. Sadly, David Garrick, the *McKay's* owner, passed away before the tug was refloated. Later in the year, the tug was donated to the Northeastern Maritime Historical Foundation and the tug is currently laid-up in need of engine repairs. This was the Foundation's first tug and if it weren't for the *McKay* the group would likely not exist. Today they have the world's largest collection of museum tugboats.

The *McKay* is powered by a massive C-6 model Kahlenberg oil engine. It was the largest engine they ever made, with the exception of the E-6, which was never mass-produced and eventually took the company out of the engine business. The C-6 is a work of art, like all Kahlenbergs. It shines of copper and brass and produces large smoke rings and a sound so distinct that any commercial fisherman on the Lakes would identify it within seconds of a quick listen. Kahlenberg engines were *the* engine for the fishing fleet on the Lakes from the teens into the 1970s. The *McKay* received her engine in 1947 after being sold Canadian, to the Great Lakes Paper Company at Fort William. They looked into repowering her again in 1964 with the turbocharged E-model Kahlenberg, but this never took place. Instead the tug was sold in 1966, at which time it was given its present name.

Not really the kind of thing you want to find when you drydock your tug. Her paper-thin hull had been patched in several places with a stick and chewing gum. Here, a stick is protruding from the engine room on the bottom of the tug. Heavy pitting from electrolysis has eaten away the tug's hull. Stray current, especially from AC power, causes electrolysis, which can rapidly speed up pitting. Normally, zinc pads are welded in various places on the hull, especially around the wheel. They will take the "hit" first and deteriorate before the hull does. Periodically they need to be changed. This is more of a problem on salt water than fresh water although a decade sitting at the dock plugged into AC shore power does a tug no favor. The *McKay* had not been drydocked in twenty years.

This image makes the engine appear small, but it's not. The C-6 in the *McKay* stands 8-feet tall and is nearly 20-feet long. The tug's chief engineer is standing above the giant flywheel with his hand on the chadburn, ready to answer the captain's bell. The engine is direct drive. If it's running, the shaft is turning. If the captain wants to stop, he rings one bell on the big engine room gong. The engineer responds by shutting the engine down by hand. If he needs to go astern, he rings twice and the engine crew responds. The engineer is busy also adjusting the timing control and fuel flow. The C-6 has glow plugs that are heated electrically to start the engine, but if one cylinder should not fire, it needs to be lit by hand with a blowtorch. This engine replaced a fore and aft compound steam engine with 15- and 28-inch diameter cylinders and a 24-inch stroke. The steam plant had been built in 1880 by the H. G. Trout Company of Buffalo.

On her delivery trip to Duluth, the *McKay* plows through some tremendous seas in the middle of Lake Superior on a stormy October 24, 2001. The tug was built by Benjamin Cowles at Buffalo in 1908. It was built for his own use and named in honor of his business partner, Walter F. Mattick. The *Mattick* was actually built with an upper pilothouse but after only a couple years, it was cut off and a low-profile house built. The tug was relocated to the East Coast for service during WW-I under the name *Merchant*. After returning to the Lakes in 1924, it was sold to the Corps of Engineers and became their *Marinette*, a name she wore until her sale to the Canadians in 1947. At that time she became the *Esther S.* and served in the pulpwood rafting trade on Lake Superior.

Huntington is powered by her original Fairbanks, Morse & Company 8-cylinder 38D-8-1/8 opposed piston diesel and giant Falk 12MB gearbox. The engine has 16 pistons, two in each cylinder, compressing against each other with the fuel injection and blow-down cocks in the center of the engine, visible in this image. These engines have a bore of 8-1/8" and a 10" stroke. The engine was also produced as a gas version (model 38DS-8-1/8) or dual fuel (model 38DD-8-1/8). The diesel-powered engine of course was most popular and still found in many tugboats today. Fairbanks and Morse built their first engine under this new company name in 1895.

Nosed in to the dock and stuck in the mud is the 1951 harbor tug *Huntington*. The tug was built by and for Ira S. Bushey's Red Star Line and served in and around the New York City area its whole life, prior to coming to the Lakes in 2004. The tug was sold by the Kosnac Floating Derrick Corporation to Ben and Sarah Fogg of Holland, MI, who intended to rebuild the tug into a live-aboard. A beautiful interior conversion did indeed take place but eventually the owners ran out of time and the tug was donated to the Northeastern Maritime Historical Foundation. The tug is pictured at Saugatuck, MI with the museum ship *Keewatin* in the background.

At Duluth, Marine Tech's tug *Miss Laura* is parked at Northland Pier waiting for another gig. The tug is a DPC tug built for the Defense Plant Corporation during WW-II, but operated by civilian crews moving oil and coal barges on the coast. There were 100 of these identical tugs built at several yards around the States. American Shipbuilding's Buffalo, NY yard built *DPC-93* through *DPC-100*. The *Miss Laura* though was built at Neponset, MA as Hull No. 1291 at the George Lawley & Son shipyard. It began life with the simple name of *DPC-3*.

The DPC tugs were mostly powered with 8-cylinder 567A engines and a Falk gearbox, which today many refer to as a "DPC" gear because of their popularity in those tugs. It was a big gearbox that could be mated with a bigger engine. Many DPCs were re-engined over the years and the *Miss Laura* was one of them. Today she is powered by a 1200-HP 12-567C with 645 components. It is pictured here still mated up with her big vertical offset 3:1 DPC gearbox. Right up front is a small heat-exchanger and a set of strainers for cooling the gearbox. Most tugs have them but many don't need them. Unless you've really got her cranked up, those big gearboxes don't really get that hot. On the side at the rear of the engine, just ahead of her clutch, is a massive air-starter bolted to the engine block.

Probably having flashbacks of her trash scow days in the New York Harbor, the *Miss Laura* has two empty dump scows on the hip and is heading back in towards the mainland from the Apostle Islands. The tug and her crew had been hauling stone from Washburn to Outer Island. Out there on nights like this, with a calm lake and a perfect sunset, there is no greater beauty imaginable.

The barge has been delivered and an exhausted engineer is taking a break on a pile of wet towline that had just been hauled in after shortening up the tow for the Keweenaw Waterway. Behind him, a few pieces of PVC piping, sliced vertically, lay on the deck. The PVC is cut and taped with lots of duct tape around the towline on the section that is rubbing on the tug's stern when towing on the hawser. This prevents chaffing of the line. After her career with Providence Steamboat, Bob Casho in Wilmington, DE fixed her up and squeezed a few more years out of her until the engine blew in 2002. Marine Tech of Duluth "got a good deal" on her in June of 2003 and had her towed down to Baltimore where she was dry-docked at General Ship. Her submarine fendering was removed and the engine was professionally rebuilt and line-bored. The tug was renamed *Miss Laura* and painted on her delivery trip into the Lakes that September.

The 85-foot DPC tugs mostly found homes with coastal ship-docking firms after the war. The *DPC-3* however, was transferred to the New York City Department of Sanitation right after WW-II. They changed her name to *DS 43* but in 1950 she was renamed again, this time to *Fresh Kills*. That was a name she wore for twenty years before being bought by the famous "Dragon Lady" and renamed *Richard K.* The tug remained in the New York City area into the early 1990s when it was resold to Providence Steamboat up in Rhode Island. In the 1970s, her original 8-cylinder engine was replaced with a 12-567BC. Here, the *Miss Laura* is underway with a barge following well behind her on a chilly and choppy Lake Superior night.

The *Chinook* rests in Escanaba ahead of the junk Inland Steel ore carrier *L. E. Block* in this May 2, 2005, photo. The tug was originally assigned the designation *CG-126* but shortly after completion became the *WYT-96*. After decommissioning from the Coast Guard, ownership was transferred to Whitehorse Marine, Inc. of Norfolk, VA. Placed on its smoke stack was a horse logo similar to that of the Merritt, Chapman & Scott Dredging Company. The Whitehorse colors are still on the tug today, as shown in this photo. The tug came into the Lakes as the *Tracie B.* Basic Marine Towing of Escanaba purchased the boat in 1994 and renamed her *Danicia*, but has only been using the tug for parts.

Chapter 4
Government Tugs: The "WYTM" Class

In the early 1930s, a diesel-electric "Harbor Cutter" was designed for the U.S. Coast Guard. These 110-foot tugboats were very traditional in appearance and built for light duty ice-breaking. The tugs were capable of busting three feet of solid ice, not too bad considering their "light duty" classification.

Initially four were built. This Calumet-class started off with the *Calumet*, *Navesink*, and *Tuckahoe*, built in 1934 at the Charleston, SC Naval Yard. That same year, the *Hudson* was constructed at the Portsmouth, NH Naval yard at a cost of $236,000.00.

These early tugs were powered by McIntosh – Seymour diesels turning General Electric generators, supplying DC power to a single G.E. propulsion motor. At the shaft was a solid 800-HP. The McIntosh engines were commonly found in HH-series Alco diesel-electric locomotives being built during the same period. A turbo-charged version was available for locomotive use but the Coast Guard tugs received a 6-clinder naturally aspirated version.

The first four tugs eventually all went civilian but the *Hudson* was the only one to hit the Lakes. It survived until 1992 when it was scrapped at Kewaunee as the *Minnie Selvick*. Last to go was the *Navesink*, which was abandoned at Panama City, FL as the *Sherman IX* in the 1980s. Finally in 2004, as part of a waterfront clean-up project, it was refloated, towed offshore and scuttled in the Gulf of Mexico as part of an artificial reef.

Based on this early design, contracts were let in 1938 for another run of the 110-footers, with slight modifications and improvements being made. The second batch of these big ice-breaking tugs differed in appearance with a more "military" look. They were heavily built and were now being equipped with armament for the approaching war. In 1939 on the Great Lakes, DeFoe Boat & Motor Works built the *Raritan* and *Naugatuck*. The same year, Gulfport Boiler & Welding Works in Port Arthur, TX built two more, the *Mahoning* and *Arundel*.

These four tugs were completed at a cost of $1,250,000.00. They were all powered by twin 567 EMD engines with Westinghouse generators and propulsion motors. The 8-cylinder diesels produced 640-HP at 740-RPM. Today, only one, the *Naugatuck* has her original power. The tug is in service for Selvick Marine Towing at Sturgeon Bay with her twin 8-567s. The two engines (serial numbers 5488 and 5499) have a build date of January 11, 1939. These very early 567s have slight variations in appearance from the typical 1940s 567A engines still found in some tugs and locomotives today.

Upon decommissioning in 1988, the *Mahoning* was transferred to the State University of New York for use as a training vessel. The *Raritan* went with it as a parts tug. Both tugs were sold surplus in 2000 and the following year cut up at the Witte scrapyard on Staten Island. The *Naugatuck* and *Arundel* are still in action on the Lakes as Selvick's *Jimmy L.* and Basic Marine's *Erika Kobasic*.

Next in line for construction were the *Manitou* and *Kaw*, both built in 1942 at the Coast Guard's own yard in Curtis Bay, MD. The *Manitou* is in civilian service on the Lakes and the *Kaw* was based in Detroit as the *Roger Stahl* until recent years when it was sold off-Lakes. It is now working from Key West, FL as the *Capt. Diane*.

Immediately following their completion, seven more were built by Ira Bushey at Brooklyn, NY.

The nice part about the *Chinook*, from a historical standpoint, is the fact she remains in her near-original configuration. Here is the standard pilothouse of a Coast Guard WYT tug. Nothing fancy, just heavily built and practical—although they had poor visibility aft, as most government tugs did.

Again, mostly original, this is a fine example of a WYT galley. The *Chinook* was built in 1943 at Bushey's Brooklyn yard. Originally the *WYT-96*, she was later reclassed *WYTM* along with the rest of her fleetmates. The tug has been dry-docked and its seacocks blanked to prevent water getting in. This greatly reduces the owner's worry over wintertime when the risk of freezing pipes is high. Frozen pipes almost always lead to sinking. So the *Chinook* is safe for the time being, but her machinery is in tough shape and her future is uncertain.

They were the *Apalachee, Chinook, Mohican, Ojibwa, Sauk, Snohomish,* and *Yankton*. They were completed in 1943-44 and along with the *Manitou* and *Kaw*, were powered by twin Ingersoll-Rand diesels with Elliot Electric Company generators and propulsion motors. The diesels were each 600-HP and the propulsion motor was good for 1000-HP.

A wonderful view, from the bow of the retired steamer *L. E. Block*, captures Basic Marine's two WYTM-Class tugs laying idle at their Escanaba yard in May 2005. The *Chinook* is on the left. To the right is the *Erika Kobasic*, which was the former USCG *Arundel WYTM-90*. She was the standard electrically propelled tug but was one of the few that had twin 8-cylinder EMD 567 engines rather than the Ingersoll-Rand diesels. Basic Marine purchased an Alco locomotive from the former Lake Superior & Ishpeming Railroad and put its engine into this tug. Today she is still diesel-electric but instead of the twin EMDs, has a single Alco model 251 turning a generator producing power for the tug's original 1000-HP propulsion motor. The *Arundel* was part of the earlier class, built in 1938 at Gulfport Boiler in Port Arthur, TX as their Hull No. 129.

The *Apalachee WYTM-71* was built by Bushey over the winter of 1942-43 and stationed at Baltimore, MD until 1984. At that time it was transferred to Portland, ME, replacing the recently retired *Yankton*. Its career in Maine was short-lived and the tug was decommissioned in April of 1986 and sold surplus. Today the tug is operational and based in Oswego, owned by Thomas Kowal. Behind the giant 110 in this June 2004 photo sits the 45-foot ex-Army ST tug. *Capt. Alix*

As of 2006, the *Mohican* is in service in the Dominican Republic as the *Catuan*. The *Ojibwa* is working from Savannah, GA as the *Gen. James E. Oglethorpe* for Crescent Towing. The *Sauk* was converted to a two-masted schooner but sank in the Atlantic Ocean in 2003.

On the Lakes, the *Apalachee*, *Chinook* and *Snohomish* can all be found in their original configuration. The *Yankton* has recently been retired from service and is for sale at Boston, also in its original state. The Ingersoll-Rand diesels are getting scarce and these four tugs hold the only eight known to be left in the world in functional condition.

These big tugs measured 110' 2" x 27' 3" x 12' 2". They normally had a 16-man crew: your tax dollars at work! These same tugs in civilian hands are operated with a crew of three.

Prior to World War II, the Coast Guard did not bother numbering any vessels that had names. They did have a contract number and, in some records, these numbers appear with the names, however unofficial they may be. The *Chinook,* for example, was first known as the *Chinook CG-126.* During WW-II, the Navy took over the Coast Guard's fleet and applied a numbering system similar to their own. They gave the small craft the length-number system we still see today and the named vessels received numbers similar to the Navy's.

These "110s" were thrown into the YT (Yard Tug) category. To distinguish the Coast Guard vessels from the Navy's, the letter 'W' was applied to the beginning of the designation. During the first two years of the war, the Navy's Yard Tugs were all classed as "YTs." As the wartime fleet saw rapid expansion, the sizes Little, Medium, and Big came into play and so the tugs were separated. The 110s were reclassed as WYTM (Coast Guard Yard Tug, Medium), even though they were larger in size than the Navy's 101-foot YTB tugs (Yard Tug, Big). And so, the WYTM class was born.

Many ask, why the letter 'W'? Naval cruisers already took the letter 'C' which would have been an obvious choice for the Coast Guard's fleet. While a letter was needed to separate the U.S.C.G. fleet from the Naval vessels, speculation is the 'W' was simply an unused letter and was so applied simply to designate their Wartime service. However, the designations stuck throughout their career and today most of the Coast Guard vessels are still classified with a 'W' type prefix.

This proud class of tugs served the Coast Guard well into the 1980s when the final bunch was decommissioned. The tugs were tremendous ice breakers and reports from their civilian owners indicate that was no joke—those remaining in service on the Lakes are *the* premier ice tugs employed in the independent tug fleets. In addition to their ice duties, the bulk of the WYTMs have been credited with heroic efforts of salvage and rescue. The *Sauk* and *Mahoning* were both at the scene of the *Andrea Doria* sinking. And to the other extreme from heroism, the tugs *Sauk, Snohomish,* and *Chinook* were all demoted to trash scow duty in the summer of 1979 during the tug strike in New York City. Coast Guard crews used the trio to shuttle barge-loads of garbage until the regular tugs returned to the gig following the strike's end.

In the late 1970s, a new ice-breaking tug was designed to replace the aging 110s. The 140-foot Bay-class WTGB tugs were mostly built at Tacoma, WA in the 1980s. This class consists of the *Neah Bay, Biscayne Bay, Katmia Bay,* and *Mobile Bay,* to name a few examples familiar to the Lakes.

Of the 17 total WYTM tugs built, most were stationed in coastal ports but today nearly all of the survivors are in service on the Great Lakes.

The *Snohomish* is under tow off Cape Hatteras on her way to the Great Lakes from Charleston, SC. The tug had been arrested a few years earlier and was tied up in Charleston seeing no action other than from giant rats, lured up the mooring lines by the smell of food still in the galley. After filling up a dumpster of trash and completing preparations for tow, the tug departed in September 2005, following Hurricane Ophelia up the coast. The tug behaved herself well on the trip, following nicely behind, almost as if she could sense she was bound for a good home in fresh water.

The *Snohomish* tow continues towards the Lakes, heading up the Hudson River through New York City, on a towline from Zenith's *Statesboro*. The *Sno*, as she is affectionately known, was built in 1943 along with six sisters at a cost of $622,677.00 each. The tug is named in honor of a Native American tribe in Washington State.

The *Sno* is waiting patiently at Troy, NY, prior to an Erie Canal passage. The tug is four feet too deep and nine feet too tall to make the canal transit. You do the math! It was a creative move, for sure. Her manager spent several days cutting everything off the top of the tug, right on down to the top of the pilothouse including a portion of the smokestack. After several trial runs of ballasting practice, the tug seemed like it may just fit and the tow departed Troy, bound for Waterford and the start of the barge canal.

On October 9, 2005, the Snohomish is at Brewerton, NY up against a railroad bridge while more ballast is added (note the suction hose off her bow). "Don't rock the boat!" is a fitting expression as the giant tug plows her way through the mud in order to pass under the bridge with less than an inch of clearance to spare. Lying on the boat deck are her upper hand rails and smokestack top, all removed for the canal passage.

Day three of the canal transit and the *Sno* is stuck in the muck. The *Statesboro* is pulling while the tug *Benjamin Elliot* (out of sight) is pushing for all she's worth. The *Sno*'s 13-foot draft had to be modified in the 10-foot deep canal by ballasting her bow down. Some areas of the canal were found to be silted in to only 8 or 9 feet. The *Sno* took on the roll of a bulldozer, pushing her way through the shallows. Ballast is being pumped out (note the discharge off her starboard bow) in order to lighten the tug to climb over this hump. The tug had just been ballasted down deep to duck the bridge pictured directly behind her.

At lock E-23 on the Erie Canal, the *Snohomish* has to pass under another low bridge, this time in the form of a guard gate at the head of the lock. Pushing the inoperable *Sno* is the tug *Benjamin Elliot*, built by Gladding-Hearn. Lock E-23 is an interesting place because its outbuildings still contain their original DC generating machinery. A fascinating tour for the engineers passing through on a diesel-electric tugboat.

Another guard gate to duck. The gate on the left was two inches higher which would have made the difference in needing more ballast or not, however that side was found to be too shallow to pass. Many people doubted a canal transit of the *Snohomish* was possible, but the tug's manager was optimistic about it right from the start. Sure enough, they made it happen. The move drew many spectators along the way on its four-day transit. These guard gates are in place to isolate sections of the canal, divert water in case of flooding or to dewater sections for maintenance.

A WYTM's engine room. Shown here, the *Sno's* main electrical board is on the upper level of the engine room, ahead of the generator room. A wonderful thing about the WYTM tugs is that their generators are behind a watertight bulkhead behind the main engine room, locking the noisy 71-series Detroit diesels in their own little "cell." This creates a quiet working environment, even in the main engine room. The big Ingersoll-Rand diesels, like most large bore, slow turning engines, are really not that loud—you *feel* what they're doing more than you hear, if you're any kind of an engineer.

The *Sno's* chief engineer and owner Chuck Cart had his work cut out for him with the restoration of the tug to operational condition. After being arrested (the tug, not Chuck) its stack covers were left off, allowing the giant Ingersoll-Rand engines to fill with water and seize. Two rainy hurricane seasons passed before the tug was acquired by the Northeastern Maritime Historical Foundation just two weeks before the tug was going to be scuttled on the reef. The tug was saved (for the time being) but still needed a costly restoration and relocation to the Lakes. Mr. Cart and his crew stepped in and took the tug on a lease-purchase, bringing it back to life over the course of a full year and a half of hard work. Today the tug is in service for Sable Point Marine of Ludington.

It is 1994 and Selvick Marine Towing has just purchased their new tug *Jimmy L.* Formerly Barnaby's *Timmy B.,* Selvick's crews are covering up the colors of the Calumet Marine Towing Company. The tug had just arrived from South Chicago to its new home at Sturgeon Bay where it is still stationed today, employed in heavy icebreaking during fit-out and lay-up of the ships. Sturgeon Bay, because of the big shipyard there, is a hot-spot for ship activity. The *Jimmy* was a first-run USCG 110-footer and is powered by twin 8-cylinder EMD 567 engines. She was the Coast Guard's *Naugatuck WYTM-92* and was one of only two built on the Great Lakes. She was decommissioned on January 15, 1979, and purchased by Barnaby the following year. *Wendell Wilke photo*

A close-up of Gaelic's *Roger Stahl* shows her original pilothouse. Her forward two portholes have been replaced with more traditional windows. The *Stahl* was built at the U.S. Coast Guard yard in Curtis Bay, MD in 1944. It was powered by twin Ingersoll-Rand diesels. Originally named *Kaw WYT-61,* the tug was decommissioned in 1980 and sold to Ed Barnaby of Chicago. In the late 1980s he started a conversion to twin screw. The project was never completed and it was finally sold to Lake Michigan Contractors in 1992. Again, the tug sat idle. In 1995 it was purchased by Gaelic Tug and the conversion was completed. Since 2003 the powerful former Coast Guard icebreaking tug has been stationed in Key West, FL, where the mild weather makes the ice-breaking duty an infrequent chore!

The *Stahl's* pilothouse interior is a work of art, typical of the beautiful conversions completed by the Gaelic Tugboat Company in Detroit. The reflection in the windows shows the backside of the pilothouse as well. The original brass-framed windows are in the front, while the side windows are obvious replacements where portholes were once mounted. The tug is now twin screw, powered by the two 12-567C engines out of the tug *F. A. Johnson*. Her original giant electric propulsion motor was left in place, for ballast, and can be found in her aft engine room.

It is January 1998 and the two-masted schooner *Allison Lake* is undergoing a conversion at the Toronto Drydock. The vessel began life in 1943 as the Coast Guard's *Sauk WYTM-99*. The tug was repowered with a Caterpillar 3512 and documented as a new vessel, built in 1998, after this extensive reconstruction of the old ice breaker. Sadly, the yacht struck a submerged object about 30 miles south of Key West in November of 2003 and sank in 3000-feet of water.

The U.S. Coast Guard tug *Manitou WYTM-60* was captured on film at New York City in 1959. These proud looking tugs served the USCG well for forty years. The *Manitou* was built in 1943 at the Coast Guard's yard in Curtis Bay, MD. She was an electric tug powered by twin Ingersoll-Rand diesels. *Robert J. Lewis photo*

Today, the *Manitou* is in service for Keith Malcolm at Port Huron. He purchased the tug in 1984 and dragged the beast through the Erie Canal, using the tug *Mohawk* to push. Back then, although still a difficult passage, the canal was dredged far more frequently than it is today due to the higher volume of commercial traffic. After arriving on the Lakes, the tug laid idle until 1996 when it re-entered service after a complete rebuild. Capt. Malcolm removed the electric propulsion system and installed a single 16-cylinder 1750-HP EMD 567C. The engine was upgraded with 645 components and swings a big wheel through a Haley reduction gear. The tug is pictured at Detroit's Nicholson Terminal on June 22, 2001.

The Corps of Engineers *Tawas* Bay began life as the *ST-2161*, built at Holland, MI in 1953 at the Roamer Boat Company (Army Hull No. 15). In the mid-1960s, the vessel was transferred to the Corps and given the name *Tawas Bay*. Upon retirement it was transferred to the USS Silversides museum at Muskegon. Still in commercial service on Lake Michigan, the tug is now Great Lakes Dock & Material's *Sarah B.* To date, the tug has spent nearly its entire life on Lake Michigan. *Author's collection.*

Chapter 5
Government Tugs: The "ST" Class

As long as tugboats have been on the scene, there has been a need for small tugs. They need to be heavy-duty with plenty of horsepower yet small enough to be used in tight quarters.

In the late 1930s, as the world was gearing up for war, the Equitable Equipment Company of Madisonville, LA designed a 45-foot tugboat which became known as the "Equity 45." They did not originate it; tugs of that design were obviously already being built on the Lakes at various yards. They were marketed to contractors mostly for light towing and dredge tending.

Up on the Great Lakes, the Burger Boat Company launched the wooden tug *Frances M. Connell* in 1934. She was built for the Fitz Simons & Connell Dredge

& Dock Company. Having the same documented measurements as the Equitable 45, the little tug is said to have been the prototype for this design.

Equitable's development of the 45-footer lead to the "Design 320" for the U.S. Army, which was mass-produced during World War II. Demand was so strong for this style boat that they built another batch in the 1950s. Oddly, Equitable did not build any of these for the Army.

Over a five-year period beginning in 1940, the U.S. Army ordered 1,686 tugboats from dozens of yards throughout the United States. Of those, 462 had the distinction of being "ST" tugs. ST meaning "Small Tug." There were many designs but the most common was the 45-footer based on the Equitable

Design 320. They are common to this day (although few remain in their original configuration). Upon retirement, these boats were hot sellers at the government auctions, being useful to marine contractors in need of a small tug that has sufficient power yet a light draft.

The majority of the Type 320 STs were originally powered by a single 6-cylinder Buda model 1879 diesel with a 2:1 MG-200 Twin Disc gear and a 44" x 36" wheel. These engines turned 990-RPM wide-open (195-HP). The end of the Navy contracts was more or less the end of the Buda Engine Company. These same engines were turned up to 1800-RPM for use in tractors but were known to come unglued when run too hard. When hot, the liners would separate from the blocks and dump water into the crankcase and dilute the oil, creating an early retirement.

During WW-II, four yards built 118 units of the Design 320 tug for the U.S. Army. With the exception of Port Houston Iron Works of Houston, TX, all of the builders were on the Great Lakes. Three shipyards constructed welded steel 45-footers for the U.S. Army. They were: the Sturgeon Bay Shipbuilding & Dry Dock Company at Sturgeon Bay, Kewaunee Shipbuilding & Engineering Corporation of Kewaunee, and the Burger Boat Company of Manitowoc. Burger had built submarines, mine sweepers, patrol boats and tugs for the Army and Navy since World War I. Kewaunee was busy in the same fashion, completing several 99-foot minifreighters for service in the South Pacific. These were powered with the big 300-HP model C-6 Kahlenberg and had a true Great Lakes-style fantail stern.

The Sturgeon Bay tugs had a "tough look" about them with slight variations in appearance from those built at the other yards. They had ST numbers in the 100s and were powered by Kahlenberg engines, typically the 150-HP B-5 model. In 1943, the firm also built one Design 320 tug for their own use and named it the *SturShipCo*. Today it is still there, in use as a shipyard tug and named *BayShip*. In appearance it is identical to the 45-foot STs.

During the Korean War when the Army was stocking-up again, another 98 units of the same design were built with slightly different fittings, but still called Design 320. Roamer was the only Great Lakes builder this time with three other yards around the U.S. building the remainder. They were: Wiley Manufacturing of Port Deposit, MD, National Steel

The *Fairchild*, another 1953 Roamer build (Army Hull No. 17) shows her owner's pride in its impressive stance. Originally *ST-2163*, this tug, like many others, saw a brief career with the U.S. Army before its transfer to the Corps of Engineers in 1961 for service on Lake Erie. Named *Cleveland* by the Corps' Buffalo district, it was transferred to the Detroit District in the early 1970s and named *Fairchild*. The tug is now a spare tug for the Corps at Duluth. Her original Buda engine has been replaced by a Detroit 8V-71. Note her curved brass window frames, top and bottom, typical of the post-war 45s. The wartime versions had perfectly square wood-frame windows.

& Shipbuilding of San Diego, CA, and American Electric Welding Company (A.E.W.) of Baltimore, MD. However, the A.E.W. tugs (*ST-2042* through *ST-2064*, Hull Numbers 116 - 138) were all built in Savannah, GA.

Roamer began their run of STs with the *ST-2016*, which was given the "Hull No. 1" designation. However, this was *not* Roamer's first hull, but oddly, part of a separate series of hull numbers applied only to the tugs built for the Army. In 1954, the Army cancelled the ST construction program. At the Roamer yard several 45-foot welded steel hulls sat in an incomplete state. The boats had been intended for the Army but were eventually completed and sold for civilian use. One such boat was the *W.P. Coppens*, which was purchased by the N.S. Mackie Company and taken to Chicago for completion. Another was the *Donald C.*, completed at Roamer for the Zenith Dredge Company of Duluth.

In addition to the 45-footers, several other tugboats were given "ST" designations. There were a number of tugs requisitioned for the war effort that had ST numbers applied to them. Also, the Transportation Corps took over a quarter of the 81-foot

Looking down from atop the crane-barge *Schwartz*, the Corps of Engineers tender *Hammond Bay* rests on the dock at the Duluth vessel yard. Built in 1954 at Roamer (Army Hull No. 24), the tug began life as the *ST-2170*. The tug was transferred to the Corps in 1962 and given its present name. It worked the Fox River area until the early 90s when it was moved to Duluth and sat ashore for the next decade, unused. The retirement of sister tug *Bayfield* led to the eventual refit of the *Hammond Bay*. Like most, the *ST-2170* was originally powered by a Buda diesel.

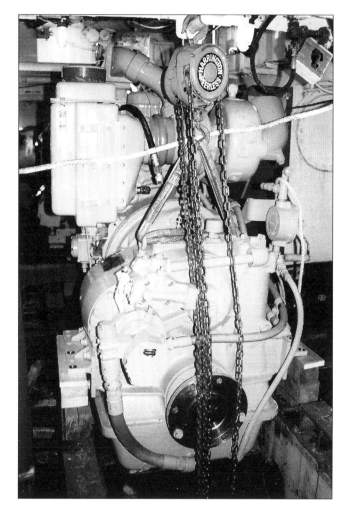

In the fall of 1999, the mothballed *Hammond Bay* received a shinny new Caterpillar 3406C diesel, replacing her old Detroit 6-71. That take-out was sold at auction and was used to repower a fish tug on Wisconsin's South Shore. The new inline 6-cylinder Cat weighs in at around 3,000 pounds, far less than its Buda and Kahlenberg counterparts. This same engine had been used in the past when several other Corps of Engineers 45-foot tugs were repowered. In this photo, chain-falls temporarily suspend the engine while the engine bed is modified to fit this new power-plant. Interestingly, about the same time, sister tug *Thunder Bay* was being repowered under ownership of Basic Marine at Escanaba. She also received a new Cat 3406. The *Thunder Bay* (ex-*ST-2168*) was Roamer's Army Hull No. 22. Initial testing showed the 3406 having too much torque for a tug of this size. So much so, that if maximum power was applied in a short interval, the tug was at risk of capsizing. Additional experimentation has proven with properly governed RPMs and the appropriate gearbox and wheel size, the 3406 is an excellent option for greatly improving the power of an ST.

Defense Plant Corporation tugs, which had all been given DPC numbers as original names. These tugs were given ST numbers in the 700 series at the time of transfer.

Other ST-type tugs were custom built under specialized designs for Army use. These additional classes were larger traditional looking tugs with an upper pilothouse and relatively tall smokestacks.

In the early years of WW-II, a 74-foot ST was developed. This Design 257 tug varied in appearance. The closest any of them came to being built on the Lakes was *ST-87* through *ST-90*, built by John Matton & Sons at Cohoes, NY, near the eastern end of the New York State Barge Canal. Today only one Design 257 tug, the *John R. Asher*, is in service on the Lakes. These 257s were powered by a single 6-cylinder, 400-HP Atlas-Imperial engine.

In the 1950s, a series of 70-footers were built. Unlike the others, this design did not originate at Equitable. Most all were powered by Atlas-Imperial, a company dating back to 1915. This was the "last hurray" for Atlas. Their engine production dwindled after WW-II due to an abundance of new war-surplus Detroit "Jimmys" that could be obtained cheaply. Only a handful were built on the Lakes. At Erie, PA, the American Boiler Works built *ST-2116* through

2130 and the lone *2198*. However, these tugs were towed out to Cohoes, NY, through the Erie Canal and completed by the John Matton shipyard.

In all, 82 of these Design 3004 tugs were constructed, including the prototype *ST-1934X*, built by Jakobson at Oyster Bay, NY. This test tug was built in 1951 but dumped by the Army early in its

This split image looking inside the pilothouse of the Corps tug *Houghton* shows that of a typical ST. Nothing fancy, just a real workhorse. The U.S. Army *ST-573* was built in 1944 at Port Houston Iron Works. This yard built *ST-543* through *576* of the 45-foot type. After her time with the Army, the *573* worked for the Corps on Lake Superior until 1992 when she was sold at auction. The tug was resold to Kehoe Marine Construction in July 2005 and is now working from Rockport, Ontario, on the Western end of the St. Lawrence Seaway. Now in Canadian registry with the same name and her Corps of Engineers livery restored, her owner reports they are loving her and she's working daily in the construction trade. Delivered to Ken and Sarah Kehoe in August 2005, the *Houghton* made the 1,430-mile voyage in 14 days, the longest trip the tug ever made under its own power. The tug was stationed at Duluth along with the *Fairchild* and *Bayfield*, which were all powered by Buda engines. The *Houghton* was the first of the Duluth tugs to receive an 8V-71 Detroit in repowering.

life. Since 1961, the tug has been operated in civilian service as the *Charleston*. It is interesting to note *ST-2199* through *ST-2201* were an obvious afterthought. These four were ordered quite late in the game and oddly one lone 107-foot LT ("Large Tug") was also in that run.

Some of the Design 320 and 3004 tugs have histories seemingly polluted by Air Force ownership. In the 1950s, the U.S. Government was experimenting with single-source procuring. For example, a run of LCMs was ordered by the Navy for the Army and consequently had *both* Navy and Army numbers assigned. The number actually welded on them by the builder was the one for whichever service needed them upon delivery. Other evidence of this is the Design 320 tugboats that came out with Navy YTL (Yard Tug, Little) numbers. A prime example of the above is the Design 3004 tug *Ann Marie*, pictured in this chapter.

It is possible that when the Air Force and Army Corps needed vessels, they were delivered directly to them, prior to an Army number being placed on their hulls. This could also explain a few gaps in numbering or specific vessels whose histories remain untraceable. Bear in mind, when it comes to researching government vessels, their stories either come with ease or with many hurdles to jump. Depending on when and where a vessel is disposed of, often all traces of their identity are destroyed prior to being placed on the auction block.

In some cases, an entirely new identity is created upon civilian purchase for the sake of obtaining a document for the vessel. One example is the Design 320 tug *TG-45*, pictured later in this chapter. Her current document (US.1126003) shows her hull number as *ST-2057*. While this is not really a builder's hull number, it is clearly a number they found on board and used it to obtain a document (proof of U.S.-build). In these tugs, there are many places where evidence of an ST number could be found, but really only one that shows a builder—a builder's plate that is usually long gone. Her document states the tug was built in Holland, MI (Roamer Boat). This is *not* true. The *ST-2057* was built by the American Electric Welding Company. A fair assumption would be that the tug was indeed *ST-2057*, a number which someone found on board, either in or on its books or perhaps welded on the hull. While filling out the paperwork for or after the GSA sale, the person at the desk knew *others* like this were built at Holland, so figured the same for this one and wrote it out as such, thus creating a history for the vessel with the stroke of a pen. Mysteries like this can be frustrating when researching vessel histories. And the rule generally is, the smaller the boat, the tougher it is to trace.

After WW-II, Equitable offered a catalog of standard sized tugs, 45-, 55-, 65-, 76-, 86-, 95-, and 105-feet in length. Many of these standardized designs were the same ones sold to the Army. The 65-footer, for example, was built to the Army Design 239 and

The tug *Lydie Rae* has pulled in for a break at the Lime Island dock on the St. Mary's River. In this June 2003 image, she is being delivered to her new owners at Cheboygan, MI. The tug began life as the *ST-912*, but like many, went to the Corps of Engineers for service on the Great Lakes after a very brief military career. On November 8, 1971, as the *Ashland*, the tug sank at Grand Marais, MN but was later raised and taken back to Duluth on board the steam derrick-barge *Coleman*. Offered at auction, the Zenith Dredge Company bought the tug for $2,540.00. It was rebuilt for service as a dredge tender for the steamers *Faith* and *Adelle*, two old derrick boats said to be named after infamous west-end Duluth prostitutes. At that time the tug was renamed *Charles F. Liscomb*, honoring the vice-president and director of Zenith Dredge.

had a 230-HP Superior diesel. Records indicate that perhaps only one of these was ordered by the Army, the *Seahound*, which today is still in service on the Great Lakes.

The largest ST ever built was the 105-foot Equitable Design 238. In addition to the ST classification, the Army also had an LT (Large Tug). The designations were more to separate harbor tugs from sea-going tugs, rather than on size alone. After all, there were LTs smaller in size than the 105-foot STs. Only four of the 105s were built for the Army and while they were never assigned ST numbers, on paper they were thrown into that general category rather than with the LTs. As an exception to the rule, there *were* ST-class tugs larger than the 105s which actually *did* wear ST numbers. A few of the wartime requisitioned tugs in the 120-foot range made the ST fleet. After the war, Equitable continued to market their standard size tugs including this 105-footer. They lacked the full-width pilothouses and the hulls were two feet wider. The *Kings Point, Fells Point, Savannah, Colonial, Lainloc,* and *Las Cocos* were examples of this type.

Prior to our involvement in WW-II, a unique looking, welded steel, 86' x 23' x 10' harbor tug was designed and built by Equitable. This "Design 327" tug was unusual, having a pilothouse spanning the full width of the main deckhouse with doors facing aft on each side, alongside the captain's quarters. This provided next to zero visibility aft. To see anything, you would have to go out one of the pilothouse doors, yet its controls were inside, center. The tugs were known to be top heavy and rolled badly in a sea. They also had no inside passageway between any of the rooms. Many considered them a poor design. With the government, however (during wartime especially) if one person said the design was great, production began! Excellent designs that received no press were consequently neglected. At the very least, these tugs were "lookers" in the minds of *some* tug buffs.

Construction of the 327 began at Equitable in 1941 and the first six went to the Coyle Lines in Texas as part of a trade to the government for barges. They were basically the seed fleet for the upcoming "DPC" tugs, built for the Defense Plant Corporation. All were given similar names: *A.H., B.T., C.T., D.D., H.F.,* and *H.G. De Bardeleben.* Oddly, one other, the *H.T. De Bardeleben,* was built by Levingston Shipbuilding. The *C.T. De Bardeleben* came to the Lakes in 1971 and was operated by Gaelic Tug in Detroit as the *Kilkenny.* From beginning to end, the tug was powered by a direct reversing 500-HP Superior diesel, turning 400-RPMs. In the 1980s, Andrie bought the vessel with the thought of repowering it but changed their mind and the tug was towed to Sault Ste. Marie and scrapped. While being cut up her pilothouse was purchased for use as a lawn ornament and may still be in the area.

The 327s did not lend themselves well to repowering. Their engine beds were too narrow. To do anything, you had to cut it all out and start over. But worse yet, they could only fit a 78" wheel.

Seven more of these 86-footers were built for the U.S. Army during these early days. The Army units were: *Col. Gambrell*, *Col. Ellis*, *Col. Agnew*, *Brig. Gen. Bellanger*, and *Maj. Harellr*. These five never had Army numbers. The final two were named *ST-9* and *ST-10*.

The Army soon adopted this tug as their Design 327 and in all, had 175 of them built. In addition to the various yards all over the U.S., two on the Lakes built twenty of them. Those yards were Kewaunee Shipbuilding & Engineering and Sturgeon Bay Shipbuilding.

The Design 327 tugs were separated in sub-classes such as 327, 327-A, 327-DS, 327-E, 327-F, and 327-JE, depending on their power-plants. Some of them had 6-cylinder Busch-Sulzer model 6DFMT-17 diesels, a Swiss take-off, built under license in St. Louis, MO. They were direct drive and had a 13" bore and 17" stroke. A small number of the 327s had a 6-cylinder Clark Brothers MD-6 diesel. Fairbanks, Morse & Company engines were used to power others of this class. Their 6-cylinder model 37E14 was used. It was a 6-cylinder engine with a 14" bore and 17" stroke. A few of these tugs had an 8-cylinder Superior-National L-08 diesel. But the bulk of these tugs had Enterprise, 8-cylinder, model DMG-38, 800-HP direct reversing diesels.

Although getting scarce, the Lakes hold more original examples of the Design 327 tug than anywhere else. The tug is a dying breed, no doubt, but for the foreseeable future a few should remain. In addition to the 327s, many fine examples of the 320 and 3004 tugs can still be found in service on the Lakes. Much of the equipment built for WW-II was considered "throw-aways," meaning if they had enough life in them to survive a few thousand hours of war-time service, they were good enough. WW-II seems to be a common division point, in terms of quality, when speaking of vessel construction. We often hear, "They don't build 'em like that anymore," talking about the heavier pre-war boats. In the 1940s though, it appears the United States ship builders did not know *how* to build a throw-away tug. These fine Small Tugs have stood the test of time and I believe it is fair to predict many will survive to see their 100th birthdays.

Parked indoors and protected from the rain and sun, the former *ST-912* is enjoying her new life with a loving owner in Harbor Springs, MI. Still in commercial service though, the 45-footer is in the marine contracting trade, tending a good size crane barge. The tug's original Buda has long since been replaced by a 300-HP Cummins NT855-M2 diesel. When Zenith Dredge went under in 1994, a new company was formed known as Marine Tech. This tug, the former *Liscomb*, was renamed *Jason* at that time and in 2001, became the *Lydie Rae*. It was sold in June of 2003 and brought to Lake Michigan. Today, as the *Elizabeth*, she is in service for Walstrom Dredge & Dock. The Burger Boat Company at Manitowoc built her as their Hull No. 651-A.

The original power for *most* of the Army ST tugs was the Model 1879 Buda engine. Since 1926, the Buda engine company had been in the diesel business, developing several unique and innovative engines in the 1930s. The tug *Escanaba* (ex-*ST-2030*, built in 1953) still has her original Buda in this July 2006 image at Joliet, IL. The tug is Hull No. 301 at Wiley Manufacturing in Port Deposit, MD. After a brief stint with the Army, the tug was transferred to the Corps in 1961 and eventually given to the Joliet Sea Scouts.

The *J. E. Colombe* (*ST-2174*) is powered by a Caterpillar 3406. Matilla Construction has owned it since about 2000, having acquired it from the National Park Service who replaced it with the *Shelter Bay*. An even earlier tug was the *Brown*, which being long and skinny, had come from the Fox River. It was powered by a 5-cylinder Kahlenberg which was saved after the tug was dismantled and later taken to Copper Harbor, MI for display.

The *ST-2057* served the U.S. Air Force after a short time with the Army. When the Department of the Air Force was established in 1947, they took over a large number of vessels from the Army. They were given an entirely different numbering system. For example, these tugs were classified as "Utility" boats and "8" was the designation for the 320s. A common Air Force name for one of these 45s would have been *U-8-* followed by the vessel's individual serial number. In the case of the *TG-45*, its military history is unknown. However, the Air Force tugboats were later reclassed as tugs and given the "TG" designation followed by the vessel's length (type) and then its serial number. So, *TG-45* is only part of the tug's true Air Force name. The tug has been repowered with an 8V-71 Detroit diesel. She is pictured here shortly before the Lake Michigan Contractors auction at their home dock in Holland, MI, summer 2004. At the auction, the tug was sold for $30,000 to the Madison Coal & Supply Company and left the Lakes.

Always a rare find is an original builder's plate attached to an ST. As the years go on, most seem to walk off on their own, or find their way under the coat of some individual who apparently was short one builder's plate on his basement wall. Here, the tug *J. E. Colombe* displays her original U.S. Army name, builder (Roamer Boat Company), Army hull number, delivery date, specification and contract number.

At Oswego the tug *Capt. Alix* is owned by Alan Hoover and is in service on the Oswego River and surrounding area. She is still powered by the original Buda diesel engine. It came into the Great Lakes in the 1990s. While its ST number is unknown, the tug was built by Wiley Manufacturing at Port Deposit, MD in 1952 for the U.S. Army. The tug was decommissioned in the 1970s and sold at auction from the Fort Eustis facility. Her purchaser had a bit of bad luck when the tug sank at the dock upon launching. It was raised and a couple of owners later, ended up in the hands of J & B Construction of Hampton, VA. This was the tug's first documented owner. The tug is named for Alix Cohen, manager of the Marina Cove Boat Basin at Hampton, VA.

The *Shelter Bay* is now operated by the National Park Service and runs between Houghton, MI and Isle Royal, on Lake Superior. The tug bears the name the Corps of Engineers gave her upon acquisition after her Army days. The tug was Hull No. 251 at National Steel & Shipbuilding in San Diego, launched in 1953. The tug was stationed at the Soo and repowered by the Corps with a Cat diesel. In the late 1990s, it was transferred to the N.P.S. and replaced at the Soo by the sister tug *Whitefish Bay*.

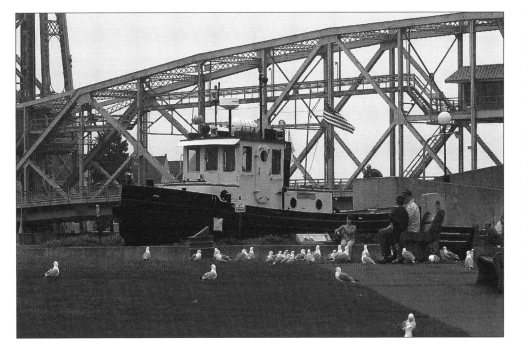

The tug *Bayfield* is on display outside the marine museum at Duluth's Canal Park by the ship canal. The famed aerial lift bridge can be seen in the background. The *ST-2023* came to the Corps in 1962. It was planted in the dirt as a museum boat in 1998. It is interesting to note that the tug *Hammond Bay* was originally supposed to be the tug placed on display. Her hull was good; the *Bayfield*'s was not. The *Hammond Bay*'s engine was weak; the *Bayfield*'s was fine. The plan was originally to swap engines, but rather, the *Bayfield* ended up as the display piece and the *Hammond Bay* received a brand new Cat diesel. The *Bayfield*'s 8V-71 is still "under the hood" today. The tug was Roamer's Army Hull No. 8, built in 1953 and retired in the early 1990's.

Another Roamer hull (Army Hull No. 16) was the *ST-2161*, built in 1953. In 1962 it became the Corps of Engineers *Oconto*. Upon retirement, the tug was placed on display at the Port of Burns Harbor where it remains today. The tug is said to have been a gift from Great Lakes Dredge & Dock to the port upon completion of the Burns Harbor facility construction. When acquired, the intention was not a display piece. The Port of Burns Harbor actually tried to use it for shifting barges, but it was found to be underpowered and eventually they gave up on the effort, plucked her out of the water and set her down by the Cargill facility as part of the landscaping. Her hull is in mint condition.

The *ST-550* was launched at Port Houston Iron Works hull in 1943. It was purchased as government surplus in 1961 by Durocher-Van Antwerp, Inc. (Durocher Dredge & Dock). As many were, the tug was repowered with a Detroit 8V-71. The vessel is still in service for Kokosing, who is now operating the former Durocher fleet. The tug was given its present name, *Ray Durocher*, in 1962. Quite obvious in this photo, the tug has received several structural modifications over the years.

Sturgeon Bay Shipbuilding & Dry Dock Company built the *ST-173* in 1943 as their Hull No. 156. This is a decent example of how the Sturgeon Bay versions had a slightly different appearance. It was transferred to the Corps of Engineers (New Orleans) after only three years of service with the U.S. Army Transportation Corps. In 1955, it came to the Lakes as a Corps tug for Chicago. Records show in 1974 it was given to the Appleton, WI Sea Scouts, although the Scouts claim to have had no such vessel. The tug was purchased by Canonie Transportation after having been ashore on display at Manistee and appropriately named *Manistee*. Documented only as *Robert Purcell*, the tug's hull shows the name *Robert W. Purcell*. Interestingly, the ashes of the tug's namesake, the late Mr. Robert Purcell, were scattered during a ceremony from onboard the tug. The boat originally had a B-5 Kahlenberg oil engine.

The *ST-175* was Sturgeon Bay's Hull No. 158 in 1943. The yard had also built wooden patrol and T-boats for the government during WW-II. This tug was declared surplus shortly after the end of the war and sold to a civilian contractor in New Orleans. In 1948, it came to the Lakes as a dredge tender for Merritt, Chapman & Scott under the name *Jane T.* It was sold to Dunbar & Sullivan shortly after, but in 1970 sold again to Luedtke Engineering and named *Gretchen B.* The tug was built with a 150-HP B-5 model Kahlenberg. When repowered with an 8V-71 Detroit, it was found the 300-HP engine could not turn the Kahlenberg wheel. The power of the Kbergs just couldn't be beat.

Purvis Marine's *Osprey* rests in their yard at Sault Ste. Marie, Ontario in this March 2000 photo. Although now in Canadian flag, it was built by Kewaunee Shipbuilding & Engineering (Hull No. 35) in 1944 for the U.S. Army as *ST-606.* It was virtually unused by the Army and transferred to the Corps of Engineers when only two years old. It was renamed *Osprey* at that time. The tug had a Detroit 6-71 diesel which was replaced in 1998 with an 8V-71. Purvis purchased the vessel in 1997. In the background of this photo, the big Purvis tugs *Anglian Lady* (1953), *W.I. Scott Purvis* (1938) and *Wilfred M. Cohen* (1948) are all laid up for winter.

Laying at Egan's yard in Lemont, IL, the former *ST-929* sits unused. Although she is documented as the *Brandon E.*, her nameboards still read *David E.*, a name which the boat gave up in 1996. The tug was Hull No. 205 at Sturgeon Bay Shipbuilding in 1945. As it seems to be with most on the Lakes, it was transferred from the U.S. Army to the Corps of Engineers. In her case, this happened in 1946 when the *929* became the Mobile, AL, district's *Heron*. The tug was resold in the 1960s and bounced around from Panama City to Chicago, finally settling down with Canonie Transportation in 1965 as the *James Edward*. For the Chicago barge service, a one-of-a-kind modification has been made: A retractable wheelhouse added! Pretty odd for a tug this small. Her original cabin is clearly visible but on her forward trunk a scissor-lift wheelhouse is mounted and the old pilothouse is boarded up. The tug's bow is built-up also with a tow-knee for pushing.

Selvick Marine Towing's *Sharon M. Selvick* has had obvious modifications to its cabin. In 1943 it was launched as Hull No. 15 at Kewaunee Shipbuilding as the U.S. Army's *ST-585*. After being decommissioned in 1949, the Corps of Engineers grabbed this one as well and worked it at New Orleans under the name *Judson*. The tug came to the Lakes for service with the Detroit District Corps in 1953. Upon retirement, the tug was donated to a Chicago-area museum group. It already had the modifications made to its cabin at that point, providing access to the quarters below via it's wheelhouse. It was sold to Selvick in 1984 and its Kahlenberg engine was then replaced with a Detroit 6-71. Today, the tug is in service at Sturgeon Bay.

The Canadian-owned, but U.S.-built, *Carolyn Jo* was launched in 1941 as perhaps the only Design 239 tug ever built for the U.S. Army. The *Major Wm. E. Warner*, as it was originally named, shows many characteristics of other Equitable designs. The classic tug was sold into Canadian registry in 1956 and eventually her 230-HP Superior diesel was replaced with a Detroit 16V-71. For twenty years she wore the name *Carolyn Jo*, but today sails as Nadro's *Seahound*. Initially, the tug was purchased and brought into Canadian registry by McNamara Marine Ltd. This was in 1956, after the tug was sold as surplus from the U.S. Army. The orange livery is that of the Pitts Engineering Company who had owned the boat for eight years already at the time of this August 1988 photo at Toronto. *Al Hart photo*

Nadro Marine's *Seahound* is certainly pleasing to the eyes. She is pictured arriving at Port Weller on August 24, 2002, employed as the stern tug on a dead-ship tow. Purchased in 1999, the tug operated under its old name, *Carolyn Jo*, for one season before Nadro Marine restored the name *Seahound*. At that time, they reconstructed the tug with twin screws powered by two 12V-71-TI Detroit diesels, greatly improving the vessel's power and maneuverability. Nadro is known on the Lakes for their vessel rebuilds and conversions. Their yard, nestled away "up the creek" in Port Dover, has seen its fair share of tugboat activity over the years. *Capt. Gerry Ouderkirk photo*

The beautiful former *ST-71* is pictured with a barge load of concrete blocks for the Major Deegan Expressway project in the 1950s. After the war, Hughes Brothers bought several of these as surplus. Within months, the *71* was transferred to Russell and became the *Russell 8*. The tug remained in the New York City area when Russell was bought-out by McAllister in the 1960s. The tug was then renamed *Reid McAllister*. It came to the Lakes in 1967 after having been bought by Gaelic Tug. It worked from Detroit and Cleveland until 1985 as their *Donegal*. Photo courtesy of James P. McAllister

The *ST-71* was one of only two ST tugs on the Lakes of the Design 257. It was built in 1943 by Platzer Boat Works at Houston, TX. The handy little tug is one of very few left in this country. Most of the 257-type survivors are overseas, left over from WW-II. Today the *ST-71* is still in service for Roen Salvage and is pictured on July 8, 2006, working on the Superior breakwall project. Its original 6-cylinder model 6HM2124 Atlas-Imperial diesel was replaced in 1973 with a fresh factory-rebuilt 850-HP Cat D-398-TA, from Barnaby's Chicago tug *Cindy B*. Barnaby had problems with the engine a few years earlier and negotiated a deal with Cat for a replacement. A brand-new engine was sent up to South Chicago for the *Cindy* and, after rebuilding the old engine, Gaelic Tug purchased it from Caterpillar for repowering the *Donegal*.

The Buffalo Industrial Diving Company of Buffalo, NY bought the *Ruby M.* from R.J. Casho Marine Towing in 2000. It had been employed in the general towing and ship assist service from Wilmington, DE. It, like the *Donegal,* was built by Platzer Boat Works at Houston in 1943. It was launched as the *ST-497.* And again like the *Donegal,* she was sold to Russell after the war and renamed *Russell 9.* The similarities continue as she too was sold surplus from McAllister in the late 1960s. As you can see in the photo, her original deckhouse has been heavily modified after a repowering. The tug left the Lakes in 2004, still owned by BidCo, and is now laying in Providence, RI, in need of further repairs. The *Ruby* is powered by a Caterpillar 398 diesel.

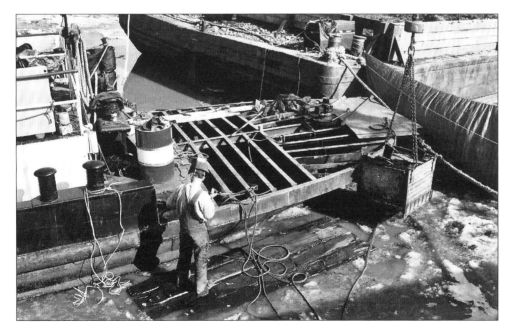

It's winter 2003 and by mid-February, the *Ruby* (BidCo dropped the *M.* from her name) was missing her stern. In this March 18 photo, crews are welding new frames and plating, replacing her old salt water-deteriorated stern section. The welder is doing a good job, working off an old barely-afloat wooden camel. Her rudder post is visible in the center, a few feet from the stern. Other tugs and barges are nestled in around her as the whole Bidco fleet is moored for winter. This lay-up period is a time on the Great Lakes where everyone pickles their fleet for two or three months and completes the annual maintenance and repair projects. Usually many of the harbors and waterways are no longer navigable due to ice conditions.

A fine example of the 1954-vintage 70-foot ST, this one has been with the Corps since 1965. It is pictured at its homeport of Kewaunee behind its riveted fleetmate *Racine*. The *Kenosha* was the Army Hull No. C-1304-24, built by Missouri Valley Bridge. Today she is the *last* 70-foot ST in the Corps of Engineers fleet on the Lakes. It seems like it happened overnight; in only a few years they made the transition from running all WWII- era STs and LTs to the more modern Navy YTBs of the 1960s. Now only a handful of 1950s Design 320 STs remain, along with this lone 70-footer, the *Kenosha*.

The *Apache* is one whose history is sketchy. Obviously an Army Design 3004, the tug seems to be one that may have been delivered directly to the Air Force, as explained in the introductory text to this chapter. To this day, her Air Force name *U.S.A.F. TG-26-1449* can be found welded on the overhang of the main cabin on the starboard side, aft. Originally, she was named *U-26-1449*, prior to the tugboats being reclassified as such, rather than "utility" boats. Throughout the 1950s and 60s she was active at the Elgin Air Force Base near Fort Walton Beach, Florida, on the Panhandle.

The *TG-26-1449* was sold civilian and documented in 1980, being given the name *Lewis Castle*. In 1998 it was renamed *Apache* under ownership of Dawes Marine at Tonawanda, NY. An aluminum retractable pilothouse has been installed behind her original. The tug was purchased by Luedtke Engineering in 2001. Now the *Ann Marie*, the former *Apache* is pictured on June 22, 2004, at Rochester, NY, mated up to a large crane barge in use on a Genesee River dredging contract. Luedtke owns an example of each major class of U.S. Army tugs, the 45-, 70-, and 86-footer, as their *Gretchen B.*, *Ann Marie*, and *Alan K. Luedtke*.

The King Company's *John Henry* is pictured at Grand Haven in July 2006. She is powered by a 940-HP, KTA-2400M Cummins diesel with a Twin Disc 6.18:1 reduction gear. The tug had been re-engined in 1983 when her 600-HP Atlas-Imperial diesel was removed. It left the government fleet in 1980 and was documented at that time as the *John Hvenry*. Originally, she was the Army's *ST-2013*, built in 1954 by Missouri Valley Bridge, as most of the 70-footers left on the Lakes were. There she was the Army's Hull No. C-1304-26. The tug is now in the construction trade on Lake Michigan.

Durocher's *General* is photographed at Ashland, WI in this September 7, 1998 photo. The tug was another Missouri Valley Bridge & Iron Works hull, built at Leavenworth, KS in 1954. Originally named *ST-1999*, she was Army Hull No. C-1304-12. The Corps picked it up, along with the *ST-2005*, in 1961 and named it *Au Sable*. It was given to a non-profit in 1984 upon retirement. However, the group turned out to be a scam, as the owner intended to use it in commercial service. The tug was taken back a year later. It had been named *Challenger* upon documenting with the NVDC. The 600-HP tug was resold at auction to Billington Contracting in 1985 and worked around Duluth a couple more years before Durocher bought it. Today the tug is still in service for Kokosing and retains its Durocher name, the *General*. The tug was named in honor of the 1900-vintage *General*, which was Durocher's first big tug and today is abandoned off Frying Pan Island near DeTour.

A cluster of tugboats is moored at the Corps of Engineers yard in Detroit. In this April 1996 photo, the 86-footer *Forney* sits among two Atlas-powered 70-footers, the *Rouge* and *Duluth*. The *Rouge* was built as *ST-2005* in 1954 at Missouri Valley Bridge & Iron Works. It was Army Hull No. C-1304-18. The Corps acquired it in 1961 and the following year picked up the *Duluth* which had been *ST-2015*, built at the same yard on the same order. It was Army Hull No. C-1304-28. Today, all three of these tugs have been retired by the Corps and sold at auction. The *Rouge* left in the late 1990s and the *Duluth* in 2001. Today, the *Rouge* remains out of service, but the *Duluth* has been repowered with a KT-38 Cummins and is in service, under the same name, for Great Lakes Dock & Materials of Muskegon. GLD&M also owns a Design 320 ST, the former *Tawas Bay*, which is featured as the first image in this chapter.

Equitable's own Design 327! They built this one, along with many others, for the U.S. Army in 1944. The *ST-707* was Hull No. 398, launched at the Madisonville, LA yard. She went to the Corps of Engineers in 1960 becoming their *Forney*, as pictured in this image, shortly after the acquisition. Aside from a few modern electronics, the tug mostly retains is original appearance to this day. Notice her lifeboat is gone and the tug had yet to receive its catwalk addition around the front of the pilothouse. On top of her smokestack, a large No. 5 Cunningham air horn is mounted. The famous Corps of Engineers castle logo was in use by the start of WW-II. Graceful tugs, no doubt. *Photo courtesy of the Northeastern Maritime Historical Foundation*

After having spent her first five years in the Buffalo District, the tug came to Detroit in 1965 and finished off her career there, finally being retired in 2003. The *Forney* was replaced by a former Navy YTB. The tug went up for auction in November of 2003 through the General Services Administration (GSA) and purchased by Arrow Mueller of New York City for $26,600. After a lay-up on the Rouge River behind Gaelic's yard, the tug was sold to another private party and delivered to Manitowoc under her own power, departing Detroit on May 2, 2004. At the time of this writing the tug is still there, offered for sale. She is pictured here in the Detroit River near Wyandotte with her cranebarge on the hip. A set of stairs and a catwalk has been added around the front of the pilothouse.

The *Forney* is still powered by her original DMG 38 Enterprise diesel. These beautiful machines are slow turning and, if maintained properly, seem to last forever. Interestingly, the *Forney* was the last government-owned Design 327 tug, bringing the end of an era that spanned sixty years. Notice on the front of the engine, an automated system has been set up, allowing control of the engine from the pilothouse. To reverse the engine, it must be shut down, the cams switched to start in reverse and then restarted. When the engine's running, the prop's turning.

After WW-II, the majority of the wartime fleet, including smaller workboats, went into lay-up at various reserve fleets. A fine example is the *ST-855*, pictured at Portsmouth, VA in 1972. This is another perfect example of how the different military branches swapped vessels. In this case, the *ST-855* had been transferred to the Navy and renamed *YTM-758*. Her windows are boarded and she's sealed up tight, ready for an extended lay-up period. For many vessels, that lay-up status continued for decades. For quite awhile the bulk of them were stored with dehumidifier systems keeping the vessels "fresh" and preventing deterioration. Of the five doors on the main deckhouse, the aft two are quarters, the center door is the engine room fiddley, fourth one up is the galley and the forward door leads to more quarters. These 327s had no inside passageway. *George Schneider Photo*

The Corps of Engineers tug *Marquette* was a favorite in the Duluth District where she served for thirty-five years. The tug was built in 1942 at Equitable under the name *Lt. Col. John H. Adams*. Sharing similarities with the smaller Design 327, her sleek lines were an impressive sight, measuring in at 105-feet in length. She was one of four sisters, the others being: *Maj. Halbert H. Noyes*, *Lt. Col. John M. Ritchie*, and *Lt. Col. George S. Gillis*. They were by far the biggest Army tugs ever built under the "ST" category. The *Marquette* is pictured in Manistee on a dredge project with a large dump scow and its tender *Houghton*, a Design 320 tug. In the early 1980s when Corps dredging decreased, the decision was made to part with several pieces of equipment. The big dipper dredge *Col. D. D. Gaillard* was one of them as was the tug *Marquette*, which often served as the tender and lake tug for that dredge. Today, the tug is working from Key West, FL as the *Mona LaRue*. *Author's collection*

The Corps of Engineers tug *Two Rivers* rests at their Kewaunee facility in February 1980. Since then, her starboard pilothouse side was extended back several feet and the door eliminated. This space was used to install a stairway leading down to the galley, creating a handy inside passageway. Albeit handy, this modification created an even worse aft visibility issue. The boat was built in 1944 by the Allen Boat Company at Harvey, LA at a cost of $256,000. It was delivered to the U.S. Army as *ST-527.* Author's collection

The former *Two Rivers* is an 86-footer in near-original condition (one of very few left in the world). Now Luedtke Engineering's *Alan K. Luedtke,* the boat is pictured at Frankfort, MI in this July 28, 2006, image. The walkways around the front of the pilothouse were add-ons that many owners have installed later in the boats' lives. Transferred from the reserve fleet at Norfolk to the Corps of Engineers in 1947, the boat was renamed *Two Rivers* and went into service from the Chicago District on the Great Lakes.

In December 1982, the *Two Rivers* was loaned to the Northwest Wisconsin Technical School on a five-year deal and wore a blue and white paint scheme for a while. The tug was used very little and eventually returned to the Corps. It was sold at auction to the Marine Contracting Corporation and was painted black and white with a "BCC" logo on the stack. Luedtke purchased the boat in 1990 but have used it very little. The tug has been in lay-up for several years now and at the time of this writing, offered for sale. She is still powered by a DMG 38 Enterprise diesel. This view of her pilothouse shows the simple interior, roll down windows, and the big direct reversing engine controls. Steering has been converted to electric joy-stick.

The *ST-500* has been in civilian service longer than any other 327 on the Lakes. Skipping the usual Corps of Engineers stepping stone, this military surplus tug was purchased in 1949 by Merritt, Chapman & Scott and named *Sherman H. Serre*. It had been built in 1944 by Platzer Boat Works at Houston (Hull No. 128). The boat was transferred to Dunbar & Sullivan in 1966. Ten years later it was purchased by Selvick Marine Towing and named *William C. Selvick*, after the founder of the company, William "Curly" Selvick. She is pictured on April 10, 1989, assisting the Canadian Laker *Quedoc* at Sturgeon Bay, WI. *Wendell Wilke photo*

Side by side at the Selvick dock, the *Susan L.* and *William C. Selvick* rest between jobs. The *William* was originally powered by a Clark diesel but has been repowered with a Cleveland diesel and air controls. It was purchased from Dunbar & Sullivan in 1977 along with the 1928-vintage tug *E. James Fucik*. Both had already been repowered with 8-278A Clevelands at that time. Notice the red lips painted on the bow fenders of the *Susan*, a nice addition to any tugboat. Also when compared with the *Susan*, note the aft mast and the roof overhangs behind the pilothouse (aside the captain's quarters) have all been cut off the *William*.

Equitable's Hull No. 400 was delivered in 1944 to the U.S. Army as the *ST-709*. It went to the Corps of Engineers in 1947 and renamed *Stanley*. It worked mostly on Lake Erie in the Buffalo District until being auctioned off in 1999 and purchased by Selvick Marine Towing of Sturgeon Bay.

In 1999, the Corps *Stanley* was renamed *Susan L.* after being purchased by Selvick. She is pictured at the Selvick dock in Sturgeon Bay in August 2003. The tug is still powered by its original DMG 38 Enterprise diesel. Light facing winches have been mounted on its bow. The forward door leads to crew quarters. The second door back leads to the galley. To get from room to room on these 327s, you had to go back out on deck and into another door—unsafe and inconvenient. Tugs today have an inside passage between almost every room, even the pilothouse. On the upper level in this photo, the back door leads into the captain's quarters. The door facing aft leads into the pilothouse and there is one found on each side.

At Sturgeon Bay, this is an interesting study of the aft ends of Selvick's two 327s. Both have been outfitted with towing machines. The *Susan* still has her original tall masts. In the summer of 2006, the *William C. Selvick* had its towing machine removed while the tug was ballasted so crews could replate the stern. The two aft staterooms were gutted and the towing machine placed inside, no longer exposed to the seas and weather.

Ryba Marine Construction purchased the *Sea Islander* from Stevens Towing in 1991. The former *ST-693* had been purchased by the South Carolina firm in 1979. The tug was built in 1944 by Decatur Iron & Steel at Decatur, AL, on the Tennessee River in northern Alabama. Ryba repowered the vessel, removing its Fairbanks Morse diesel, replacing it with a 1200-HP Cummins model KTA3067M diesel. On its first job of the 2006 season, her engine blew and that spring the tug was repowered with a Cummins KTA50C producing 1600-HP at 1900-RPM. The tug is used for lake towing, moving construction barges and dredging equipment between job sites. Some of her doors have been blanked as a much-needed inside passageway was created. Steps leading up the forward end of the main deckhouse provide a handy access to the pilothouse, rather than its original ladders on each side. A more streamlined smokestack was constructed upon repowering and is out of view in this image, snug behind the pilothouse.

This fascinating image of Barnaby's former Army tug in action on the Calumet River reveals many modifications, yet many original ST features as well. Her hull, cabin, and fiddley skylight are classic "327." A push knee has been extended on her bow stem. Her smokestack has been cut off and a low-profile canaller stack constructed. A retractable pilothouse has been installed and its front is obviously salvaged from the ST's original house. These modifications were made when the vessel was purchased by the famous Ed Barnaby of South Chicago. Built in 1945 as the *ST-880*, it was Sturgeon Bay Shipbuilding's Hull No. 185. The tug went to the Corps in 1947 and was their *Avondale*. Calumet Marine Towing (Barnaby) purchased the vessel in 1964 and ran her up the river right to the shipyard at St. Louis for repowering. The horsepower race was on in Chicago and the old 650-HP Busch-Sulzer diesel would not do. Barnaby had the yard install a 1350-HP 12-cylinder 645-E2 EMD, brand new, straight from the factory at LaGrange, IL. The tug was renamed *Adrienne B.* and entered service in South Chicago where it can still be found working today. The guides for the retractable house were made out of 6 x 6 timbers against channel iron and flat plate. Under the house, towards the starboard side, folding guides can be seen, which hold the hoses and wire bundles leading from the controls to the systems down below. This keeps everything neat on the way up and down, preventing pinching or tangling.

The *Adrienne B.* was renamed *Old Mission* in 1995. John Kindra (Kindra Lake Towing) bought-out the Barnaby operation in 1992 and eventually renamed all the tugs. When the tug was converted to a canaller, its original captain's quarters were saved and rest in their yard as a storage shed. In this image, her house is all the way down. The overhang on the main deckhouse has been cut away and made flush. On her bow, facing winches have been installed. Quite rare, this tug has ancient heavy steel half-doors down the side. This is the only 327 tug in service on the Lakes which was actually *built* on the Great Lakes.

The tug *Arthur* was photographed at Ashtabula on June 17, 1998, enjoying a weekend off from her construction trade. The 53-footer was built in 1929 by John H. Mathis at Camden, NJ for the U.S. Army Corps of Engineers. As their tug *Dover*, the tug worked the Philadelphia District until being sold at auction in 1968 to the Long Island Towing Company. It was documented as the *Dover* but was resold in 1975 to the Barker Boys Towing Corporation, becoming their *Margaret Barker*. In the mid-1980s, it came into the Great Lakes. It became the King Company's first *Julie Dee*. Her current owner, Polovic Construction, purchased the vessel in 1992 and applied her present name.

Chapter 6
Small Tugs

In addition to the Army's "ST," a whole other world of tugs exist, probably thousands of them in this country alone that can be classified as "Small Tugs." The only requirement is they must be… well, *not big.*

Performing many of the same tasks as tugs discussed in every other chapter in this book, these tugs are often times just scaled down versions of a larger prototype. The bulk of these tugs are used in the construction trade for moving scows in areas requiring light draft. A whole series of similar looking 40- to 45-foot dredge tenders are used for just that, tending

dredging operations—moving crews and provisions to and from the floating plants and repositioning scows and dredges.

Duluth's Marine Iron & Shipbuilding designed a grocery launch hull in the late 1920s that was modified in the mid-1930s as a towing vessel. The Corps of Engineers ordered several of these 40-footers for use as tugs classified as "survey launches" or "dredge tenders," depending on how they were outfitted. About a dozen of them were constructed between 1935 and 1937 and it is believed all of them remain in existence at the time of this writing. This design

The graceful lines, wooden windows and riveted cabin of the tug *Elizabeth* shine through in this action shot at the annual Detroit River tugboat races. It was built by the Alabama Drydock & Shipbuilding Company in 1935 at Mobile, AL for the Corps of Engineers as their *Chester*. The 65-footer was completed at a cost of $50,058.32. The tug was stationed at the C & D Canal through the duration of her career and when retired, stayed in the area working in Philly under her new name, *Elizabeth*. The tug is powered by a pair of inline 6-110 Detroits with a common gearbox in the center; this engine had replaced a 6-cylinder Winton diesel. Alexander Winton was a pioneer in the diesel engine business, building his first in 1913. Winton built the first V-12 diesel two years later. The company was purchased by General Motors in 1930 and their 2-stroke V-12 led to the development of the 278A and 567. Electro Motive was purchased by G.M. the same year they acquired Winton. Today the *Elizabeth* retains its original appearance and is in service for owner Paul Vassall in Detroit.

was soon replaced with the larger, more powerful 45-footer that was beginning to be mass-produced by the Equitable Equipment Company in Louisiana.

Similar to the Army Design 320 discussed in Chapter 5, the "Equity 45" was a 45-foot dredge tender built until about 1970. Early prototypes can be linked directly to the Great Lakes shipbuilders throughout the 1930s, proving the design was public domain. Manitowoc Shipbuilding produced more of them than any other yard during this time. Equitable built many of the "State-Class" tenders for Great Lakes Dredge & Dock, all with U.S. state nicknames applied. An interesting twist of fate is that one of the very earliest prototypes for the Equity 45 was GLD&D's *Prairie State*, built in 1934 at Duluth by Marine Iron—the very yard that was building the

40-foot dredge tender. And oddly, it was completed before the first 40-footer ever came off the line!

Other examples of this class built on the Lakes include: the *Bay State* (built at Manitowoc in 1930), *Beaver State* (Manitowoc, 1935), *Stella B.* (Manitowoc, 1935), *ManShipCo* (Manitowoc, 1936), *Hoosier State* (Ft. Wayne, 1938), *Erich R. Luedtke* (Manitowoc, 1939), *Badger State* (Chicago, 1947), *Wolverine* (Toledo, 1952), *Garden State* (Toledo, 1956), and the *Peach State* (Sturgeon Bay, 1961). Of course, many more of the GLD&D tenders such as the *Empire State* and *Buckeye State* were standard Equity 45s. Many of these are still in service on the Lakes today.

But back to the basics, most of these handy little tugs can be operated by one person, two at the most. They can be easily started and made ready to use in just a matter of minutes. Other than the classic model bow designs discussed above, some are built as towboats, with flat-bow barge-like hulls, normally twin screw. These tugs have a very shallow draft and are handy for light-duty construction jobs such as marina or private dock and seawall construction projects.

Other little tugs can be found at the Great Lakes shipyards, used for light-duty towing or tending repair projects. Often built with a tug appearance, these shipyard tenders are more often found in the repair trade, moored alongside ships with their welding equipment going full bore. Since Great Lakes shipbuilding activity is only a fraction of what it used to be, the shipyard tugs are more or less a thing of the past, but a few remain. They are normally built in-house at the very yard where they are needed.

A number of the tugs in this size range have been converted from other types of vessels or the opposite may be the case—they are sold upon retirement and converted at that time into something other than a towing vessel. Fish tugs are the most common source of hull for a towing vessel conversion. Interesting how it came full circle, since the early fish tugs were converted from tugboats.

Some of the smallest tugs are the "alligators" which

The *Avery Bay* has been given a classy paint scheme and was captured in action at the Soo on September 6, 2004. The tug was built by Sturgeon Bay Shipbuilding in 1942 for the Corps of Engineers. Originally named *Moore*, the tug was retired in 1973 after being holed out and sunk in Burns Harbor. It was towed to South Chicago and donated to the Sea Scouts who used it to replace a 36-foot former Coast Guard motor lifeboat. The Murphy Engine Company agreed to donate a fresh engine to replace its 5-cylinder direct reversing Fairbanks Morse engine that was damaged from her time underwater. In 1976, the new Murphy went in and as a "thank you" the tug was renamed in honor of that little 4-cycle Murphy that brought the tug back to life. Sailing under the name *Little Murphy*, the tug was eventually transferred to the Michigan City Sea Scouts where it worked until another sinking on February 10, 2002, due to improper lay-up. The tug was made operable again but declared surplus. Finally in late 2003, it was sold to a private party who in turn sold it into Canadian registry. Today it can be found at Sault Ste. Marie as the *Avery Bay*. *Jon LaFontaine photo*

The Corps of Engineers tender *Col. J. D. Graham* was built by Spedden Shipbuilding at Baltimore. Although they shared no similar appearance, the *Graham* was a sister to the *Captain A. Canfield*, delivered to the Corps from Speddon one year prior to the *Graham's* completion in 1924. Army Corps tugs were generally ordered from the district headquarters, so it was rare that other districts built boats of the same type unless word got around that they "got a good one." The *Graham* was one of those which received several design modifications and improvements and by the time she was outfitted for delivery to the U.S. government, it was a first class tug and the envy of many. *Author's collection*

Today, the 53-foot *Col. J. D. Graham* is alive and well, working for Ferriss Marine Contracting out of Detroit as the *Magnetic*. The Corps retired the tug from the Detroit District in 1965 and it was purchased at auction by the Nicholson Terminal on the Detroit River. It was renamed *Nicholson* and used around the area as a yard tug for their terminal and shipyard. Ferriss removed her Kahlenberg oil engine upon purchase in 1977 and installed a pair of Detroit 6-71s. In 1983 she was given her present name, a name which had been adopted from Magnetic Street in Marquette, MI. In this photo, she is spotted on the Rouge River, holding the 335-foot Andrie tank barge *A-410* up against the wind while crews get their mooring lines out. *Capt. Wade P. Streeter collection*

are used in logging operations on the Canadian side. These sturdy little tugs were built with large winches inside that can be used to winch themselves up on land, often times between lakes, while gathering pulpwood to build log rafts which would then be towed by bigger lake tugs to the mills. Many of these remain although very few are in service.

And due to the size of the small tugs, quite a few have been purchased by private parties and restored as pleasure boats. Some retain their tugboat appearance, others do not.

These small tugboats can be found in nearly every harbor around all the waters of the Great Lakes. Some have classic lines, others are just flat, boxy looking push-boats. Whatever their design, like all tugs, they are powerful boats, ready to tackle the tasks they were built for.

One historic little tug on Lake Superior is the former Marine Iron & Shipbuilding's yard tug *Billy M.*, now stationed at Bayfield. She is pictured amongst the retired fish tugs in this June 2001 image. A smokestack is visible and since this image was taken, the tug has been outfitted with an even larger stack. However, as built in 1929, the tug had no smokestack. Marine Iron built the tug for their own use as a shipyard tender used during side-launches of new hulls and miscellaneous duties. Originally it was named *John Abernethy*, in honor of the yard Superintendent. Shortly before WW-II, the tug was renamed *Swan Larson* after a succeeding superintendent. In 1950, the Meierhoff family bought out the yard and the tug was given its present name. It is powered by a 4-71 Detroit diesel.

In the mid-1930s, Duluth's Marine Iron & Shipbuilding developed a small "tender" for the Corps of Engineers based on the hull of their 35-foot grocery launches built in 1929. This new hull was almost identical in appearance, but 40-feet in overall length. It became the dredge tender of the day but was soon replaced when an abundance of war-surplus Army Design 320 tugs hit the market. Several of these well-built little tugs were completed and today, although long retired from the Corps, many still exist. This 1937 photo shows one nearing completion at the Duluth shipyard. A worker is cooking rivets on her back deck while two others are busy stitching her cabin together. The background is cluttered with Great Lakes Dredge & Dock dredging equipment. *Author's collection*

The *Oatka* was recently launched at Marine Iron and is out for a cruise in the Duluth harbor. The Corps tug is powered by a 60-HP direct reversing 2-cylinder Fairbanks, Morse & Company engine at the time of this photo. That engine would later be replaced with a Grey Marine 6-71. The tugs in this class measured 40-feet long, 10-feet wide, with a draft of 4' 4" and weighed roughly 12 tons. The *Oatka* was the sixth hull built by Marine Iron in 1937. As completed, these tugs were sent to Corps Districts all over the U.S., east of the Mississippi. The *Oatka* was the one tug that remained in the port she was built, leading to the "Oatka-Class" designation, even though she was not the first one constructed. *Author's collection*

For a good portion of the *Oatka*'s career, she was stationed at Warroad, MN on the Lake of the Woods. It had been moved there overland from the Duluth vessel yard in two pieces; cabin on one truck, hull on another. Today the tug is owned by Bruce VonRiedel and can be found stationed at Cornucopia, WI on Lake Superior's South Shore. This photo shows clearly her new smokestack position and new stack itself, no longer the rounded style she was built with. Also it is interesting to note her stack colors, which were later adopted by the Zenith Tugboat Company, owned by the same family. The riveted cabin really sticks out as well. Her aft towbitts have been removed and a ventilation hatch has been cut into the back of her deckhouse.

In the 1970s, the *Oatka* retired to Detroit and was given to the University of Wisconsin at Superior. Eventually her 6-71 blew and they put in a small turbocharged Perkins diesel. Her name was changed to *Gull*. In 1990, the tug was sold surplus and redocumented as the *Miss Midway* for the local Midway Oil Company. The tug was used very little and after a few years sold to VonRiedel, who restored its original name. Portions of her hull that were wearing thin were cut out and properly replaced in 1995. She is shown in this image amongst her bigger sisters at the Duluth Timber dock in June 1999. The bumboats are moored directly behind her as well as the tugs *Seneca* and *Essayons* along with all the retired Zenith Dredge steamers.

This is an interesting photo to compare to the construction image. In Maine, the *Johnny* was retired and scrapping had already begun when John and Rachel Collora rescued the historic old tug and took it home to rebuild. Even for an experienced steel worker and machinist, John has taken on quite a project. New decking, frames, hull, and cabin plate are being installed. The project began in the mid-1990s and is nearing completion at the time of this writing. The tug is a 1937 Duluth-built Corps tug that went simply by the name *E 15*. At Eastport, ME, the *Johnny* was operated by Passamaquoddy Towing Services. *Photo courtesy of John Collora*

Marine Iron was obviously proud of their work because in addition to a builder's plate inside, nearly all their bitt-caps and hatches inside and out are cast with the builder's name. Oddly, the *Oatka* has a 1934 builder's date on her deck hatches. There is speculation they were either leftovers at the time of construction or added later, replacing her original worn-out hatches with new old stock.

The Canal Corporation's *Dana II* is ashore at their old facility at Syracuse, NY. This facility has since been demolished and a new one built near Three Rivers Junction. The *Dana* was the former Corps tug *Rostock*, based at Albany until 1981. After WW-II the tug was repowered with a Detroit 6-71, which lasted until 1985 when it blew and another one was put in. Winter is approaching in this Fall 2000 image and her 6-71 has been removed in preparation for another repowering.

A crane is setting the tug *Rambler* back into Lake Champlain after a bottom job at Burlington, VT. The tug was originally the Corps of Engineers *NY 15* based on the Long Island Sound until the 1950s. It passed through several owners in the Jersey area and finally in 1967 was purchased by the Lake Champlain Transportation Company which operates the ferries. The tug was given the name *Rambler* which it wore until 1995 when it was sold surplus and went into Canadian registry in the Ottawa area. In 2001 the tug was sold to Jim Gibbons of Bow, WA and trucked all the way to the West Coast. It was renamed *Vintage Lady* and repowered to steam. No, that's no typo—today the tug actually has a boiler and a functioning 2-cylinder fore and aft compound steam engine that had once powered a fish tug on Lake Superior. *Photo courtesy of Bill Dumbleton*

One of the first Marine Iron 40-footers, the *Manitou* is pictured in Port Clinton on August 25, 2002. The tug was retired from service in recent years and has been offered for sale. *Manitou* is powered by a Detroit 6-71 diesel. The Gray Motor Company of Detroit introduced the marine 71 engine in the 1930s. Later built by General Motor's Detroit Diesel division, production was stepped up for use in Army tanks in 1940 and by the end of WW-II, more than 180,000 Detroit 71s had been built. Since their beginning, they have been popular in small tugs and are still common power for them today. *Roger LeLievre photo*

Nelson Construction's tug *Eclipse* has not strayed far from her birthplace. She is another of the 1937 Marine Iron 40-footers delivered to the Corps of Engineers. The tug was purchased from an Ashland-based private party in 1976 by the Nelson family and has been in service for them ever since. Today the tug is based in LaPointe, WI, in the Apostle Islands and engaged in the construction trade. When purchased by Nelson Construction, the tug had a 60-HP Kahlenberg engine which was replaced in 1978 with a Detroit 6-71. In the early 1990s, her superstructure was replaced which is obvious in this photo. Her 6-71 was replaced with an 8v-92 Detroit.

Although her nameboards read *Haskal*, the spelling of this tug's name is officially *Haskell*. This was her original name when built in 1936 at Marine Iron in Duluth. As a sister to the Oatka-class, this tug is a "stretch version" with an extra long cabin, an extra window in her pilothouse and an extra port-hole in her engine room trunk. It was classified as a "Survey Launch" rather than "Tender" like the others. The 40-foot hull has retained its original appearance. She is powered by a Detroit 6-71 which, due to a few engine failures, is actually the third 6-71 this tug has used. Originally it was powered by a 6-cylinder, four-cycle, high speed, Fairbanks-Morse model 36A diesel, complete with reduction gear. This was a unique and innovative F-M design.

Bay Shipbuilding's tug *BayShip* received its name in 1968 when the Sturgeon Bay Shipbuilding & Drydock Company became Bay Ship. The tug was built by the yard in 1943 as the *SturShipCo*. With just a quick glance, it is apparent that she was built from the Army Design 320. The tug is used around the shipyard to help positioning ships during dry-dockings. She is pictured here clearing ice for Inland Steel's *Joseph L. Block*.

Port Houston Iron Works built the 45-foot *L. D. No. 617* in 1943 for the Corps of Engineers, Louisville District at Kentucky (hence the "L D" in its name). The tug is an obvious take on the Design 320 ST. Its original 5-cylinder A-model Kahlenberg engine still powers the tug today. She is pictured ashore at the McMullen & Pitz yard in Manitowoc. After retirement from the Corps, she worked as the *Marilyn* for the Alton Barge Service in Illinois for two years before coming into the Lakes in 1956 for her current owner. At that time, the tug's name changed to *Erich*. The tug has been out of service for ten years now but thankfully in good hands; an owner who cares enough not to cut it up for scrap.

Resting on the banks of the Cuyahoga River in this June 18, 1998, image is the retired Great Lakes Dredge & Dock tender *Prairie State*. The tug has been in this state, engine-less, for a decade now. It was built in 1934 at Marine Iron & Shipbuilding of Duluth. This very well may be the first steel 45-footer of the style that led directly to the development of the Equity 45 and later the U.S. Army's Design 320.

Calumet River Fleeting's *Tommy B.* was built in 1938 but not registered until 1949 by the Great Lakes Dredge & Dock Company at Chicago. She was their *Hoosier State* and had been built at Fort Wayne, Indiana, by the American Steel Barge Company. The dredge tender was sold to the Calumet Towing Corporation in 1961 and after a refit was renamed in honor of Tom Barnaby. The tug saw less service in the 1980s and by the 1990s was retired, sitting in the reserve fleet of the Calumet River Fleeting Company. In October 2006, the tug was purchased by Zenith Tug of Duluth and renamed *Park State*. The tug was gutted while still at the Cal Riv yard and reconstructed by Zenith crews. Today she is powered by a Detroit 6-71 and stationed at Manistee, MI.

The *Chris E. Luedtke* was built in 1936 by and for the Manitowoc Shipbuilding Company. As the *ManShipCo*, she was used as a yard tug at their Manitowoc Shipyard, much like Sturgeon Bay's *SturShipCo*, pictured earlier in this chapter. The tug was sold to Luedtke Engineering in 1980 and is in service as a dredge tender. She is pictured nestled in amongst the rusty old barges, all iced over and laid up for winter. Tracks in the snow down her deck are from the resident kitty who was guarding the iron that winter. Her classic wood-frame windows and the two-chime Kahlenberg air horn were standard on the tugs of her day.

The Great Lakes Dredge & Dock tender *Beaver State* is captured in action on the Cuyahoga River on May 30, 1985. The 45-footer was built by Manitowoc Shipbuilding as Hull No. 281 in 1935. Throughout its life the little tug has worked mostly at Cleveland. It, along with many others, was eventually sold to Lake Michigan Contractors. Today the tug is owned by MCM Marine based at Sault Ste. Marie. *Al Hart photo*

The *Buckeye State* rests ashore below the 92ⁿᵈ Street bridge over the Calumet River in South Chicago. This was the yard of the Great Lakes Dredge & Dock Company but today is home to Dawson's Holly Marine Towing. The tug is an Equity 45 built at Madisonville in 1951. After GLD&D, an excursion boat operator purchased the vessel shortly before he was murdered, after which his boats were sold out of the area. Lake Michigan Contractors ran the tug as a dredge tender again before selling it to Buffalo Industrial Diving out east. The tug is still in the Buffalo area, privately owned under the name *International*. *Al Hart photo*

It's April 2006 and MCM Marine's dredge tug *Peach State* is resting inside their big dump scow *No. 55*. The Keweenaw Peninsula is on the horizon as the pair, along with another scow, are under tow across Lake Superior after completing a project in Duluth. The *Peach* was built in 1961 at Sturgeon Bay for the Great Lakes Dredge & Dock Company of Chicago. In the mid-1990s, the tug was sold to Lake Michigan Contractors. MCM acquired the 45-foot tender in 2001 and kept her original name.

The famous Toledo boat-builder Hans Hansen constructed the *Wolverine* in 1952. The 45-footer is shown here in TNT Dredging colors, underway at Allouez on August 30, 1998. Superior, WI can be seen in the background and behind it is Duluth, MN (that big hill back there). The *Wolverine* is powered by an ancient Caterpillar diesel and was built for Price Brothers on Lake Erie. It was later bought by LaCrosse Dredging on Lake Michigan and in the 1980s went to the King Company, tending the dredge *J. W. Wilkinson*. This was one of TNT's first tugs and remains in their fleet today.

In the midst of the MCM Shipyard at Sault Ste. Marie, the yard tug *Mackinaw City* rests in this May 2005 image. The tug was built in the 1940s and is powered by a 6-cylinder Murphy diesel. It was previously owned by the Twin City Dry Dock, the former name of the shipyard now owned by MCM. This cute little tug is uded to shuffle vessels around the shipyard, assist in dry-dockings and help out local construction projects where MCM-owned barges are employed.

At the Kadinger yard in Milwaukee, the small tug *Mermaid* awaits her next job in this July 1993 image. The tug was built by and for the Calumet Shipbuilding & Dry Dock Company in 1936. As the *Calship I*, the tug worked around the shipyard and tending vessel repairs on the Calumet River. After the yard closed, the tug was sold through many owners in the Chicago area and finally ended up in Milwaukee in the construction trade.

Today the *Mermaid* is owned by a private party in Milwaukee and after a restoration is now in immaculate condition. Her old wheel has been polished up and new pilothouse windows installed. Originally it was powered by a small Kahlenberg which was replaced with a 6-71. The 71 was also replaced and the tug is now powered by a Detroit 6-110 diesel with a 3:1 Allison gear. The firing order of the two inner cylinders is interchanged on a 110 and with a load on, they run extremely smooth. Smoother than a 71-series, however, the much lighter weight of the 71 vs. the 110 brought the 71 into the spotlight in highway applications and the 110 was eventually phased-out.

It's winter lay-up in Sandusky and the George Gradel Company's yard is packed with barges and tugs. On the left is their handsome 56-footer *Mighty Jimmy*, which was built in 1945 by American Electric Welding at Baltimore. This firm also built ST tugs for the Army in the 1950s. She came to the Lakes as the *Ariel*, working for McHugh's on the Erie Canal from Syracuse. Originally she was Chesapeake Lighterage Company's *C. L. No. 1*. The tug is powered by a pair of Detroit 4-71 diesels. To the right is the famous little *Timberland* which was first documented in 1946 but rumors have dated the boat a bit older. It gained fame during its employment with the Consolidated Paper Company as a log-rafting tug. Originally she was the *George F.*, built at Grand Haven by and for George S. Ver Duin as a fish tug. It was converted to a towing tug when Consolidated purchased it in 1956.

At the Zenith Dredge yard in Duluth, their small dredge tending towboats *John V. II* and *Melvin L.* are ashore with an uncertain future in this May 1990 photo. The 40-foot tugs were built in 1941-42 at Valley Parks (St. Louis, MO) by the Barbour Metal & Boat Works for the U.S. Army Corps of Engineers. There were three sisters, the *Beebe* (*Melvin L.*), *Blake* (*John V. II*) and the *Bogus*. The first two were bought by Zenith in 1962 and taken to Duluth for use tending their dredges *Faith* and *Adelle*. Today, the *John V. II* remains in Duluth owned by a private party while the *Melvin L.* was renamed *Don L.* and went to Florida to work for Lake Michigan Contractors. *Jon LaFontaine photo*

American Marine's twin screw construction tug *Defiance* is pictured at Indiana Harbor on January 13, 2002, laid up for winter. The handy little tug is used for moving a crane barge and repositioning during sheet-piling and dock reconstruction jobs. The 45-footer was built by Harrison Bros. Drydock at Mobile, AL in 1965 but brought into the Lakes via the river system in the 1980s. American Marine also owns the big DPC-Class tug *Alice E.*, which was built as the *DPC-32* during WW-II. Both are in service on Lake Michigan. *Tom Hynes photo*

Calumet River Fleeting's push tug *Matador VI* is pictured at the KCBX terminal in South Chicago on April 19, 2002. The tug was owned by KCBX but operated by Cal Riv for nine years. Owner John Selvick bought the tug in the summer of 2006 and had the boat overhauled at the Chicago Dry Dock. It is powered by a pair of 600-HP Cummins diesels and has twin flanking rudders. Scully Brothers Boat Builders built the 42-foot tug in 1971 at Stephensville, LA. Her original name was *Miss Josie*. Today it is used for shifting barges on the Calumet River and has been renamed *Little Nicky*, being a smaller version of the *Nicole S.*, Selvick's big canaller which was retired in 2005.

The twin screw *Muskegon* is moored alongside the old hydraulic dredge *J. W. Wilkinson* at Monroe, MI on June 19, 2004. The tug was built by the Lemont Shipbuilding & Repair Company at Lemont, IL in 1973. It is powered by a pair of D379 Caterpillars. The 75-foot tug was built for Bultema Dock & Dredge and eventually went to Canonie and finally Andrie in 1987. King bought the tug in 1994 but sold it off-Lakes in 2005, purchasing the larger *Maribeth Andrie* instead. Today the *Muskegon* is operating from Fort Pierce, FL as the *Elizabeth Anne*.

The Kremer Motor Company built the tug *Kendee* in 1960 at Gulfport, MS. It came right to the Lakes, stationed at Milwaukee through the 1970s. In the 1980s it became Barnaby's *Michelle B.* Holly Marine Towing bought the tug in 1998 and renamed it *Debra Ann*. Her original Detroit diesels were yanked out and a pair of 290 Cummins put in. In 2002, the tug was sold to TNT Dredging and the 290s came out and a set of 400-HP turbocharged 855 Cummins put in their place. In 2003, TNT renamed the tug *Joyce Marie*, after the owner's mother. The tug left the Lakes with a dredge and the larger tug *Bonnie G. Selvick*, all of which are currently stationed in Mississippi.

DeFoe Boat & Motor Works built the 55-foot tug *Jack Boyce* in 1943 at Bay City for their own use. The shipyard tug was sold in 1978 and went into service in the construction trade on Lake Erie. Today the boat is owned by Shoreline Constractors of Westlake, OH, and goes by the name *Eagle*. It is pictured here made up to a cranebarge at Rocky River on April 18, 2003.

It is December 1998 and the *James Wrickey* is inbound Rochester working against a sea with a scow on gatelines. The 42-footer was built in 1935 by Sparling Shipbuilding at Astoria, NY. Originally named *Susquehannock*, the tug is said to have been built with a steam engine but refitted with a diesel engine after ten years. *Jason R. LaDue photo*

Sturgeon Bay Shipbuilding & Dry Dock built Durocher's *Betty D.* in 1928. The 55-foot tug was sold to Edward Gillen in 1932. At that time it was renamed *Killarney*. After three years it was again sold, this time to the Luedtke Engineering Company at Frankfort. They applied the name *Karl E. Luedtke*, a name she has now worn for over seventy years. In the background of this interesting photo sits an old Northwest crane, one of Luedtke's steam-powered derrick barges, and a car ferry. The classic old *Karl E.* looks just the same today. *Author's collection*

Durocher's *Joe Van* was built in 1905 at Buffalo. The former steam tug has been reconstructed over the years and no longer retains its original appearance. The tug was photographed at Manistique on June 19, 1997. The 50-foot boat was originally named *Theodore E. Cowles* and kept that name through its 37-year ownership with the powerplant at Niagara Falls. It was purchased by Durocher Dock & Dredge in 1955 and given its present name, honoring Joseph Van Antwerp. After repowering from steam, the tug received a pair of Detroit 6-71s side-by-side into one gearbox. Later, the tug was one of the first in the country to receive a Series 60 Detroit.

Julio Contracting bought the harbor tug *Joey Haden* in 1972 for service around the Keweenaw Peninsula. The tug was renamed *Julio* but saw very little service and mostly languished at their Hancock, MI yard. The tug was built in 1941 at Port Arthur by Gulfport Boiler & Welding Works. It was originally named *Mary Louis* and served in the Gulf oil trade. The tug was renamed *Venus* in 1948 but changed the following year to *Joey Haden*. It wore this name through the 1970s working for W. D. Haden and the Seaway Barge Lines.

Finally in 1998, the *Julio* was dragged ashore and scrapping began at Julio's yard. Conveniently, scrap is a large part of what the contractor handles, so the rusting hulk was right at home. Her large direct reversing Atlas-Imperial engine was removed in addition to other machinery and the cabin and bulwarks. Scrapping stopped with the hull though, and at the time of this writing the 71-foot steel hull still remains as pictured, on the beach at Julio's.

The tug *Islay* was built by Alexander McDougall's American Steel Barge Company shipyard in Superior, WI in 1892. McDougall designed and constructed the famed "Whaleback" freighter on the Great Lakes. The tug was built with a beautiful wood cabin and used not so much as a towing vessel but as a showpiece for the yard and its executives and clients. Later the tug's cabin was removed and a steel one put in its place, when the tug entered service as a grocery launch in the Twin Ports. After WW-II, the tug went to the Ashland area and was renamed *Bayfield*. Jumping ahead through a tremendous pile of history, the tug was found more or less abandoned at Milwaukee by 1982. Local tug operator Greg Stamatelakys acquired the tug and spent the next twenty years restoring the old tug, reinstalling a vintage Kahlenberg oil engine. In 2004, Greg donated the tug to the Northeastern Maritime Historical Foundation. He remains on board with the organization as project manager. The tug is scheduled for continued restoration and relocation to the port where she was born.

The small tug *Escort* is standing by for the launch of the Coast Guard's latest acquisition, the new icebreaker *Mackinaw*, named in honor of the old one which performed so well over the course of sixty years. The *Escort* was built in 1955 by and for Peterson Builders shipyard at Sturgeon Bay. In 1996, the tug was sold to Basic Towing of Escanaba, on this day is providing the support tugs during the launch at Marinette Marine in Marinette, MI.

As the new *Mac* slides down the ways, three Basic Marine tugs have hold of a long line that runs through a connection on the dock so that when the tug pulls, it actually pulls the ship in the opposite direction—back towards the pier. On the other end, the Design 320 ST tug *Krystal* is at work. And standing by is the big WYTM-class *Erika Kobasic*. Peterson Builders also built and operated the tug *Escort II* (1969). Both the *Escort* and *Escort II* are 47-feet in length. The *Escort II* was sold in 1996 and is owned by Selvick in Sturgeon Bay as the *Cameron O*. Both tugs were built for shipyard use. That yard went under, the tugs were sold, and ironically both remain in the shipyard tending service, just at *different* shipyards.

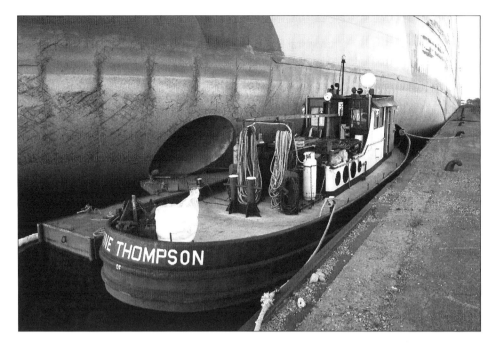

The Fraser Shipyard tug *Maxine Thompson* is parked under the bow of the giant 1000-foot ore carrier *Edwin H. Gott* who is in port for thruster repairs. That big "hole" in the ship is the bow thruster tunnel, which is normally under the water. The ship has been pumped out high and dry, exposing the tunnel so shipyard crews could get inside to make repairs. Several of these handy little tugs were built by and for the shipyard in the 1950s for ship-side repair jobs with thrusters, rudders, or changing propeller blades. The *Maxine* was built in 1959 as the *Susan A. Fraser* and is powered by a 300-HP Cummins. They are well equipped with torches and welding machines, enabling their crews to tackle almost any job.

For years, a rusted old 70-foot junk tugboat with no name sat along the banks of the Rouge River. But if you looked closely, you'd see it wasn't a junker after all. The thing was brand new! The tug was the project of Elmer Dean and took him a long time to build. But he passed away before the tug was ever completed and so the tug sat. Finally in 1998, Darin Gabriel was able to purchase the hull and finish it, naming it in honor of its builder who never got to see it run. *Al Hart photo*

Now completed, the *Elmer Dean* took first place in the 451-1000-HP Class in the 2001 Detroit River tugboat races. In this June 23rd photo, she is approaching the finish line with her flags flying proudly. The tug took second place overall in the races that year. She is powered by twin Allis-Chalmers diesels.

The 38-foot tug *Julie Ann* always makes for some exciting Kodak moments in the annual tugboat races. From the looks of this photo, I can't tell who's more frightened, the tug's engine or the two guys who just went over the stern! The skinny old tug is plowing through the wake of the big tugs that have pulled ahead in the lead. The river is really churned up during this event. The *Julie Ann* is owned by a private party in Harrison Township, above Detroit. It was built in Erie, PA in 1934.

Sitting ashore in Thunder Bay, Ontario, is the 1950-built *Pat D.* The tug was completed at Goderich, built at the Matieson yard. The 40-footer is currently owned by Pierre Gagne Contracting. The wall of steel behind her is the 730-foot hull of the 1964-vintage Laker *Saguenay*, which was towed overseas for scrap not long after this photo was taken. The *Pat D.* is powered by a Detroit 180-HP 6-71 diesel. In this photo, repairs have led to her smokestack being cut off and it can be seen lying on the stern deck.

Gradel's yard in Sandusky used to be a division of Erie Sand and home to the sand-sucker *John Emery*. In this June 2004 photo, two tugs rest in the sand-sucker's old spot. On the left, the *Pioneerland* is a sister to Gradel's other tug *Mighty Jimmy*, pictured earlier in this chapter. Not a sister in looks or type, but a former owner's fleetmate. In 1947 it became the Chesapeake Lighterage Company's *C. L. No. 2.* The tug was originally Maritime Oil Transport Company's *Bessie R.*, built at Houston in 1943. Next to this 58-footer is their *Mighty John III*, which interestingly was a Canadian-built tug. For a United States document to be issued, an exception is needed to the Jones Act, which prohibits any vessel being used commercially that was not built in the U. S. This very old piece of legislation was put in place to protect American shipyards, among many other reasons. The *John* began life as the *Niagara Queen*, built in 1962 by the old Toronto Drydock Company. Her sister, the *Breaker*, is stationed at Buffalo. Both tugs were originally owned by Ontario Hydro and later sold to the New York State Power Authority.

The Mollhagen family of St. Joseph, MI had their fish tug *Herbert* built in 1908 at Johnston Brothers in Ferrysburg. The 70-foot tug had a more traditional tugboat appearance, much like the early days of fish tugs on the Lakes. It was steam powered and had a steam net lifter on her starboard bow. In 1918 it was renamed *H. Ewig* for Ewig Fisheries on the Wisconsin side of Lake Michigan. The tug was sold to Love Construction in 1939 and refit for use as a towing vessel under the name *Roy R. Love*. She was resold to Bultema Dock & Dredge in 1966 and renamed *Charlevoix*. After the Canonie years, the tug was purchased by Dennis Rapp for service on the rivers within Chicago. It was used very little and remained in the Canonie green and white with the restored name, *Roy R. Love*.

In 1950, the *Love* was repowered with a 250-HP C-5 Kahlenberg. There are only a couple C-model Kahlenbergs known to be in existence in the world. This monster 5-cylinder is quite simple in design, but a true work of art. Visible on the front end of this engine is her vertical gear-driven fuel pump and governor. Moving the speed control lever will extend or withdraw the single cam, allowing the governor to change the stroke of the fuel pumps, which in turn increases or decreases the speed of the engine. The single cam creates perfect firing order through its control of the five separate fuel pumps. Also visible in this photo are her engine controls which control fuel timing, engine speed and starting lever for reversing. A sprocket and chain-drive leads up to the pilothouse where a control has been installed, allowing the captain to control his own engine. Some say it worked, but really, these engines were designed to be hands-on engineer operated.

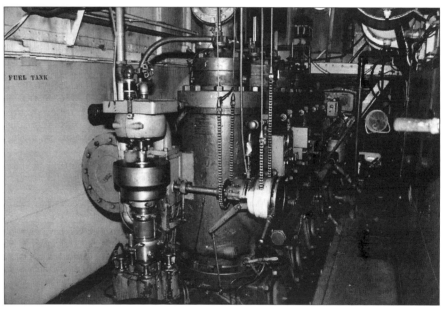

Zenith Dredge's old tug *Sea Bird* is ashore at their Duluth yard in the 1970s. The tug has lived on like a cat with nine lives but has certainly burned up a few of them through multiple collisions and sinkings since its construction in 1900. It was built by Johnston Brothers as a steam passenger ferry for use at Grand Haven. After WW-I it was converted to a fish tug and in 1939 Ernest LaPointe brought the tug up to the Bayfield area from Waukegan. It was powered by a huge cast iron 3-cylinder Wolverine gas engine with a 48-inch flywheel. When fishing slowed down, the tug was no longer needed and in 1971 LaPointe sold it to the Zenith Dredge Company. They rebuilt into a towing vessel. It has gone from steam to gasoline to her current Cummins diesel and is privately owned in the Ashland area. *Author's collection*

It's low tide at Troy, NY and an impressive line-up of tugs rests in the fog. Up front is the *Mavret H.* followed by the *Benjamin Elliot*, *8th Sea*, *Snohomish*, and the *Sharon Elizabeth* alongside a cranebarge. The *Mavret H.* was built as a classy-looking fish tug in 1927 at the Great Lakes Engineering Work's yard in Ashtabula. It was requisitioned during WW-II by the U.S. Coast Guard and after the war transferred to the City of Cleveland for conversion to a fire tug. It was converted to a towing vessel after twenty years and has passed through many owners, all opting to keep its original name. The tug is powered by a rare 3-cylinder 268A Cleveland diesel and is in beautiful condition.

Ryba Marine Construction's tug *Venture* rests above the Soo Locks in this June 1997 image. The tug was built in 1922 at Buffalo as the fish tug *E. W. Sutton.* It was converted to a towing tug in 1952 and given the name *Venture.* The tug has had its share of bad luck over the course of its 85-years in existence. She has sunk numerous times, twice in the same year near the compensating gates above the Soo Locks. They say it's bad luck to rename a vessel, so perhaps another renaming will reverse the damage done—in 1998, the tug was rebuilt and renamed *Amber Mae,* in honor of the owner's daughter.

Roen Salvage has their little tug *Timmy A.* ashore in this February 1998 image at Sturgeon Bay. The tug was built as the *Calhoun* by M. D. Moody & Sons in Jacksonville. The 35-footer was given its present name in 1964 when it turned ten years old.

At her berth along the St. Clair River, the 1923-vintage *Canadian Mist* is enjoying the view. The 50-footer was built by the Interlake Engineering Company at Cleveland for the Standard Oil Company. An ironic beginning, as she poses by the $1.39 gas sign in this July 2002 photo. Originally, the tug was named *Red Crown* and built to fuel yachts in the Cleveland area. It was converted to a towing vessel in 1974. *Al Hart photo*

The tug *West Wind* is a 1941-built 60-footer that came into the Lakes from the New York area. Its original name was restored in 1961 but for a while was the *Russell 2.* The tug was built by Lester Alexander at New Orleans. A Detroit 12V-71 has replaced her original 225-HP Atlas engine. The tug is pictured at the Bidco dock at Buffalo in March 2003.

On display at Owen Sound is the "Alligator" tug *Ancaster*. She was built locally at Russel-Hipwell in 1951. These little 25-footers were used in logging operations, most often found on inland lakes. The 20-HP *Ancaster* was built for the E. B. Eddy Company at Hull, Quebec. A cage can be seen around her propeller, to protect it against debris and logs, by which the tug is usually surrounded when working.

At Hudson, Ontario, the old *C. W. Cook* is pulled up and out of service. It is pictured there on March 17. 2003. The tug had been purchased from Charles Cox by a mill who intended to use it in the logging trade. Castings on her tow-bitts indicate the tug was built at Buffalo, NY in 1924 by the H. G. Trout Company. Her superstructure has been heavily modified. *Robert B. Farrow photo*

Two Russel Brothers tugs are laying in the Purvis Marine scrap yard. They are not going for scrap; just laid up awaiting their fate. On the left is the *Waub Nav No. 1*, which was built in 1941 as the *Alona* for the Abitibi Power & Paper Company. To the right is the *Goki*, built in 1940, also for Abitibi. In the background, the Paterson Steamship bulk freighter *Quedoc* is under the knife, beached stern first and scrapping well underway.

Another Russel Brothers hull, the 65-foot tug *Ottawa* was built in 1943 for the Canadian government. It was powered by a Vivian diesel which was replaced in 1975 with a pair of Cat D353s. The tug was renamed *Lac Ottawa* in 1957 and given its present name in 1966. In this June 2004 photo, the *Colinette* is ashore at the Nadro Marine shipyard in Port Dover for reconstruction. The tug was originally a low-profile harbor tug but in late 2001, it was pulled out and rebuilt to a more traditional looking two-deck harbor tug. This project was never completed and the tug was eventually reconstructed, as shown in this photo, to a yacht with the aft pilothouse.

Built for the Canadian government's Department of Transport, the *Welland* was launched in 1954 at Russel Brothers in Owen Sound. For most of its life the 86-foot tug has worked in and around the Welland Canal. The tug was repowered in 1995 with a Detroit 12V-149, replacing an English 600-HP Crossley Brothers diesel. *Author's collection*

The *Westpete* was built by the Erieau Shipbuilding & Drydock Company at Erieau, Ontario, in 1953. The tug worked as a tender for the Consolidated West Petroleum Company of Toronto into the 1970s. *Capt. Gerry Ouderkirk photo*

Another dredge tender, the *Halton,* is ashore at Whitby in this March 1999 image. It was built in 1942 at Muir Brothers Dry Dock in Port Dalhousie. Originally she was named *Workboat No. 8* for the Canadian Dredge & Dock Company.

Similar in design to the previous tug, the *William* is photographed ashore at Hamilton in March 2002. She is a Canadian dredge tender, built in 1938 by and for the Canadian Dredge & Dock Company as their *E. Smillie*. It worked under the name *Workboat No. 6* from 1946 through the 1980s. Eventually CD&D sold the 35-footer to Bermingham Construction of Hamilton. *Jason R. LaDue photo*

A large crane has picked the *William Rest* out of the water at Toronto for repairs in this March 1, 1999, photo. The tug was built at Erieau Shipbuilding for the Toronto Harbor Commissioners in 1961. The unique-looking 65-footer is powered by a Caterpillar D-398 diesel.

Canadian McAllister's big tug *Daniel McAllister* was donated to the Montreal Maritime Heritage Society in 1998 for intended museum use. It has yet to be restored as shown in this 2004 image at Montreal. The 115-foot tug was built by Collingwood Shipbuilding in 1907 as the *Helena* and doubled as a harbor/lake tug, spending a good portion of her time on the St. Lawrence Seaway system. After a 1955 sinking at Chicago, the tug was renamed *Helen M.B.*, rebuilt, and repowered in 1957. Her steam engine was replaced with a 12-cylinder A-block EMD. In 1965, McAllister Towing purchased the tug. The following spring, her crew overhauled the machinery at Kingston and the tug then ran light to Montreal where further repairs and modifications were made. On October 1, 1966, she was rechristened *Daniel McAllister*, honoring a son of the owner. *Robert B. Farrow photo*

Chapter 7
Lake Tugs

The Great Lakes have been home to large over-lake tugs since the beginning of commercial navigation. Heavily built tugboats, strong enough to withstand the harsh weather conditions, are needed to haul barges, dead ships, and log rafts across the Lakes. Many styles exist and can be found in action on all five lakes. Their appearance is widely varied, like any other type of tug. These boats built for towing from port to port, across the lakes, are usually quite large and have plenty of horsepower to handle a heavy tow in a rough sea—which can pop up quickly on the Lakes. Fuel capacity is another concern, espe-

cially when you're burning as much as 200 gallons an hour pushing a load across the lake.

The U.S. Army Corps of Engineers has been operating lake tugs since the beginning. In recent years, the tug of choice was the former U.S. Army LT ("Large Tug"). Three sisters, the *Ludington*, *Lake Superior*, and *Nash* were all in service on the Lakes. In the 1990s, all three were replaced by more modern tugs and as luck would have it, all three were preserved as museum vessels.

These "LT" tugs were the Army's Design 271, measure 113-feet long, and are powered by massive

Enterprise direct reversing diesels. Enterprise has been in the engine business since 1886 and built their first diesel in 1920. The LTs had about the biggest Enterprise you'd find in a tugboat. In all, there were a total of 16 tugs in this class. The prototypes appear to have been the tugs *Dauntless No. 14* and *Dauntless No. 15*, built before WW-II at Jakobson's. The *No. 15* became the Army's unnumbered LT, *Col. Albert H. Barkely* and after the war went to Curtis Bay Towing. After the *14* and *15*, Jakobson built *LT-1* through *LT-8* and down in Tampa *LT-18* through *LT-23* were built by Tampa Marine.

The *LT-18* became the Corps tug *Lake Superior*, which today is on display at Duluth. It was Hull No. 1 at Tampa Marine, which actually appears to be their first vessel construction. This is a different firm than Tampa Shipbuilding, which was constructing vessels for the Navy during WW-I.

The Corps used their three LTs for over-lake towing, hauling large dredges and crane-barges between job sites in their district. They served well and were comfortable sea tugs, according to former crew members. The *Lake Superior* was replaced by a more "modern" former U.S. Navy YTB ("Yard Tug, Big") and there are mixed reviews but a common opinion seems to place the *Lake Superior* as the better boat.

In recent years, several ex-Navy YTBs have come to the Lakes to work as lake tugs for the Corps. Now, instead of the three LTs, the *D. L. Billmaier* (ex-*YTB-799*), *Cheraw* (ex-*YTB-802*) and the *Demolen* (ex-*YTB-829*) are in this service on the Great Lakes. These tugs were built in the late 1960s and into the early 1970s and have plenty of power as harbor tugs. At Navy surplus auctions, they are popular with the East Coast tug companies for conversion to tractor tugs. They were built tough and are wide enough to convert to twin screw. Several of these 109-foot YTBs were built on the Lakes. They were either powered by EMD or Fairbanks Morse diesels.

Other former military tugs exist on the Lakes in barge service. After WW-II, the Army and Navy had more tugs than they had employment for and many were discarded through surplus auctions. Civilian towing companies bought them and several made it into the Lakes. Chicago's Hannah Marine operates several ex-Army 149-foot LTs which were originally powered by 3-cylinder Skinner Uniflow steam engines. One such tug, the *Bloxom*, still exists in her original configuration, abandoned in New York

The United States Shipping Board ordered a series of 48 ocean-going 150-foot steam tugs for WW-I. The 150-footers were so big that they were a choice candidate for diesel repowering and many lived on. Several were built in Superior, WI at the Whitney Brothers yard. The tug *Butterfield* is one in this class, although built off-Lakes at Bethlehem Shipbuilding in Elizabeth, NJ. In 1922, the tug was purchased by Consolidated Paper and went into the pulp rafting trade on the Lakes. She is pictured as Canonie's *John Purves* in December 1983. *Author's collection*

By the time the Second World War rolled around, the tug was needed again and consequently requisitioned by the U.S. Army, becoming their *LT-145* from 1942 until 1945. It was then purchased back by Consolidated. Roen Steamship bought the tug in 1957 and gave her the name *John Purves*, not to be confused with the Canadian *Purvis*. The *Purves* was then converted to twin screw using the pair of EMD 12-567A LST engines and gears out of the barge *Solveig* (a former *LST*). She is pictured here in Bultema colors. *Author's collection*

City's Witte boneyard. The tugs operated by Hannah have been through extensive refits and have all been repowered to diesel. They are all engaged in the oil trade across the Great Lakes.

A few ex-Navy ATA ocean-going tugs have found their way into the Lakes and are still in service. Some old steam tugs have survived after conversion to diesel and still serve as lake tugs. Others remain as museum vessels.

Other large multi-purpose tugs are in the overlake trade; they were built on the Lakes for well-known dredging contractors. Contractors such as Great Lakes Dredge & Dock and the Merritt Chapman & Scott Corporation have had big tugs built for the same use as the Corps of Engineers, to haul their own equipment from job to job. For a long time the Roen Steamship Company and Great Lakes Towing were leaders in lake towing.

Modern twin screw tugs have also been brought into the Lakes by Hannah, Andrie, McKeil and others to use pushing barges. Twin screw tugs are often required in the oil trade so most of these high-horsepower relatively new tugs (built in the 1960s and 70s) have that duty, mated up with a single tank barge. The bulk of these tugs are built off-Lakes.

Some huge ATB tug/barge units are in service on the Lakes, replacing aging steamships. Often the barges are converted *from* the old steamships, whose fresh water hulls are perfectly fine. Worn steam machinery and a large operating crew is a turn-off to the companies who consequently opt to refit the ship as a barge. Massive tugs are built to fit into a notched-out stern on the old steamship hull (or in many cases, a newly constructed barge to fit into a specific trade). Van Enkevort Tug & Barge, Interlake Steamship, K & K Integrated Logistics, Upper Lakes Towing, Great Lakes Fleet, Lower Lakes Towing, St. Mary's Cement, and the LaFarge Corporation are a few firms that operate large bulk cargo tug/barge units. Many of the tugs employed in this trade are locked into their barges with a pin system and are rarely separated. Some of them tend to be virtually useless as tugs on their own, having been built to serve a specific purpose.

So the next time you think you're watching a ship pass, take a closer look at the boat's stern. It just may be a tug pushing a barge!

Eder Barge & Towing ran the *John Purves* in the 1970s and in 1980 the tug was bought by Canonie Transportation. After Andrie demoted the tug to a "back up boat" in the mid-1990s, her fate was sealed. She did a few odd jobs, the last big tasks being cold December tows. She moved the steamers *J. L. Mauthe* from Superior to Bay Ship in 1996 and the *Milwaukee Clipper* from Chicago to Muskegon a year later. This wheelhouse interior shot shows the *Purves* on December 31, 1996, at Duluth, waiting for a break in the weather in order to depart with the *Mauthe* in tow. The pair had actually tried departing a day earlier but ice conditions stopped them just outside the piers and they had to turn back. The tug was donated by Andrie Inc. in 2003 for museum use in her former hometown. The impressive *John Purves* was restored to the Roen Steamship colors in 2006 and is now on display as a museum vessel in Sturgeon Bay.

With the exception of a classic hull, what you see in this photo is more or less a replica. The steamer *James Whalen* was acquired by Thunder Bay interests for restoration as a museum vessel. She serves that function today and is a beautiful display piece. However, her stack and wheelhouse had to be reconstructed from blueprints and photographs. They had been removed in 1959 when her 1896 fore and aft steam engine was replaced by a 16-278A Cleveland diesel. Her cabin was rebuilt with a more streamlined design. The 1905-vintage steamer was built by Bertram Engineering at Toronto. It was towed to Thunder Bay, engineless, in 1992 but had actually been working off-Lakes since the 1970s as the *Denise V.*

Up a hidden creek above Detroit rests the old 120-foot Canadian tug *Queen City*. The tug was built at Kingston in 1911 for the Public Works Department of the Canadian government as their *Polana*. The tug originally had a large steam engine but was repowered in 1957 with an Alco diesel. The boat was converted to a floating restaurant at Windsor in 1982 and served that purpose for twelve years. The classy interior of this old riveted tug is still intact and serves as a "club house" for her owner.

The former Corps of Engineers tug *Ludington* rests in her berth at Kewaunee on August 7, 2003. The tug was retired two years prior and given to the city for use as a museum vessel. It began life in 1943 as the U.S. Army's *Major Wilbur F. Browder* but was renamed *LT-4* after a short time. This "LT" was Hull No. 297 at the Jakobson Shipyard in Oyster Bay, NY. She was built with an Enterprise diesel which has a bore of 16-inches and a stroke of 20-inches. The monstrous engine produces 1200-HP, but a very large 1200 compared to today's high-speed diesels. Interestingly, three identical ex-Army 113-foot LTs ended up on the Great Lakes and all three became museum vessels after retirement from the Corps. The *Nash* (ex-*Major Elisha K. Henson*, ex-*LT-8*) is on display at Oswego. This was Hull No. 298 at Jakobson.

Another of the LTs is on display in Duluth. The Corps' *Lake Superior* started out as the Army's *Major Emil H. Block* as Hull No. 1 at Tampa Marine Corporation. It was renamed *LT-18* in 1947 and three years later transferred to the Corps of Engineers and given its present name. The tug, like the other two, is powered by a 1200-HP Enterprise. Upon retirement, her spare parts were sent to Oswego for the *Nash*, since that group actually operates theirs from time to time.

The former Corps of Engineers tug *Washington* is pictured at the Basic Marine shipyard in 2005. The tug began life in 1952 as U.S. Army *LT-1944*, part of the 107-foot class of "Large Tugs." It was built by Avondale Marine Ways in Louisiana. They were powered by direct drive Fairbanks Morse 37F-16, 6-cylinder, 1200-HP, slow-speed diesels. The Corps acquired the tug in 1962 and kept it working on Lake Erie until 2000 when it was sold to Dawes Marine on Lake Ontario. The tug was documented as the *Sea Chief* but worked very little before being purchased by Basic. The tug was dry-docked and her sea cocks blanked for long-term lay-up. At this time, her future is uncertain.

The Navy's *Chetek YTB-827* is pictured in action at Baltimore. In the background over her stern, the Curtis Bay Towing tugs *Town Point* and *Cavalier* rest at their home dock. The *Chetek* was one of many 109-foot Navy YTBs built on the Great Lakes at Marinette Marine. She was launched as their Hull No. 307-12 in 1973. It returned to the Lakes in 1996 after being acquired by the Corps of Engineers, replacing the tug *Washington* in the Buffalo District. The Corps kept the name *Chetek* for a while but it has since been renamed *Koziol*. In 2005, the tug's ownership was transferred to the St. Lawrence Seaway Development Corporation and, along with the barge *Sampson*, the pair is now stationed on the U.S. side of the Seaway. The tug is powered by a 10-cylinder 38D-8-1/8 opposed piston Fairbanks Morse diesel. *Ted Stone photo*

With a freshly painted hull, the *USS Natchitoches YTB-799* rests at the Newport, RI Naval yard on September 5, 1971. Her name can be seen welded across the stern but not yet repainted. The 109-footer was built for the U.S. Navy by the Southern Shipbuilding Corporation at Slidell, LA (Hull No. 79) in 1969. Many of these identical tugs were built on the Great Lakes at Marinette and Sturgeon Bay. The *Natchitoches* was stationed in the northeast, working from Newport and Boston until being transferred south and finishing off her career in North and South Carolina. It was given to the Corps of Engineers in 1995 to replace their ex-Army LT tug *Lake Superior* at Duluth. Orders from the Detroit District issued July 7th of that year read, "Prepare and crew one *YTB-799* tugboat from Charleston, SC to Duluth, MN… and tow Cranebarge *Huron* from Detroit, MI to Duluth, MN, enroute." Crews did just that and today the tug is the Duluth-based *D. L. Billmaier. Ted Stone photo*

The Corps lake tug *D. L. Billmaier* is pictured in the Fraser Shipyard dry-dock on May 1, 2003. It was drydocked with its accompanying cranebarge *H. J. Schwartz.* The pair was new to the Duluth Corps of Engineers in the 1990s, the *Schwartz* having been new construction and the *Billmaier* transferred from the Navy. Today the pair is in service on Lake Superior and Lake Michigan performing breakwall repair and general marine construction projects for the federal government. She is powered by a turbocharged 2150-HP 12-cylinder EMD 645.

The Detroit tug races have just concluded and the party has begun over at Windsor. The big Corps tug *Demolen* came into the Lakes in 2001 after its transfer from the Navy. As the *Metacom YTB-829*, she had worked the submarine base at New London, CT since her construction in 1974 at Marinette Marine.

Ice is packing in around the former *Gaelic Challenge* at Burns Harbor in this December 28, 1995, photo. The tug has been renamed *Frankie D.* by Eagle Marine Towing for service between Chicago and Burns. Two tugs were purchased from Gaelic in order to begin a new towing operation. The service never really got off its feet and in 1997 both tugs ended up in lay-up at 92nd Street in South Chicago and owned by Glenn Dawson. The *Gaelic Challenge* was built by Jakobson in 1944 for the U.S. Army as the *LT-643*. The 130-foot tug was powered by a Fairbanks Morse diesel with a 16-inch bore and 20-inch stroke. This was removed in 1979 shortly after Allied Towing of Norfolk purchased the tug at auction. They had a 1950-HP EMD 16-645-E7 installed. The tug was used in the Chesapeake area under the name *Taurus* until being laid up in the mid-1980s.

Gaelic purchased the *Taurus* in 1989 but really had their work cut out for them. The engine was stuck and the tug had many bugs to work out. They did their usual top to bottom overhaul of the tug and ran her on the Lakes, especially for ice work, until her sale in 1995. After Eagle Marine shut down, Dawson did a once-over on the tug, getting her up to code and then in 1997 sold her to McKeil Marine under the name *Dawson B.* It ran out to McKeil's Hamilton yard in brown primer with the name stenciled on, as seen in this January 1998 photo. The tug was rebuilt by McKeil and an upper pilothouse added to see over tall barges. It was renamed *Doug McKeil* and re-entered service later that year. In August of 2005, the tug was sold again for off-Lakes use, but still in Canadian flag with the name *Western Tugger*.

The *Mary Page Hannah* was laid down at Levingston Shipbuilding in Orange, TX in 1944 as the U.S. Navy's *ATA-230*. It was intended for service in Russia on the Lend-Lease program. However, the contract was cancelled and the tug remained incomplete until 1949 when visiting officials from General Motors noticed the hull. They ordered it to be completed as a flush-decker and had it outfitted with twin Cleveland 12-278A diesels with a single screw electric drive. Delivered in 1950, the tug was named *G. W. Codrington*, in honor of George Codrington, Vice-President of G.M.'s diesel engine division. Mr. Codrington had started with Winton Diesel in the teens and was named president in 1928. Two years later, Winton was bought out by G.M. and in 1938 the name was changed to Cleveland Diesel. The diesels developed by General Motors were a huge part of our success in WW-II. The tug *Codrington* was purchased by Great Lakes Dredge & Dock in 1951 and later owned by Stender, Hannah and finally Selvick, who today operates the tug from Sturgeon Bay. In this image, she is dragging the retired Lake Michigan car ferry *City of Midland 41* out of Ludington on October 1, 1997. If the tug was completed as ordered, she would have been a twin to the Lakes' own *Tug Malcolm* and the *Undaunted*. As an interesting side note, the ferry pictured was cut down to a barge and today her notch tug is the *Undaunted* (*ATA-199*), a would-have-been "sister" to the *Mary Page Hannah*. *Steve Elve photo*

Hannah's *Kristen Lee Hannah* is pictured at Milwaukee on September 19, 1997, with the tank barge *Hannah 5101*. The tug was built at Point Pleasant, WV in 1945 for the U.S. Army as their *LT-815*. The 149-footer is one of three identical ex-LT tugs that Hannah currently owns. The *815* was sold at auction in 1964 and became the *Henry Foss*, working on the West Coast. It came to the Lakes in 1984 as the *Kristen Lee* but the full name was applied ten years later. The tug blew an engine in 1999 and entered lay-up at South Chicago. Today the tug remains in lay-up but is officially named *David E.* Here's where the story gets interesting: A year later, Hannah purchased the big towboat *David E.* from Egan Marine. Months later, Egan purchased another towboat, the *Irving Crown* and since they no longer had one by this name, they renamed that one *David E.* Hannah took their new tug *David E.* and, to

keep the name on a functioning boat, renamed it *Kristin Lee Hannah*. They couldn't have two of them on the books like that and instead of wasting a good name on an out-of-service tug, they swapped names and gave their old *Kristin* the new name of *David E.*

The *Kristin*, or perhaps we should be calling it the *David E.*, is powered by two 8-cylinder 2500-HP Nordberg diesels. The port side engine is down and torn apart to locate the problem. This view is looking down from the upper engine room. These tugs are truly *ships* in terms of engineering. The massive Nordbergs stand two stories tall. Originally, this tug and her two sisters, the *Mary E. Hannah* and the *James A. Hannah* were all powered by 3-cylinder Skinner steam engines.

Capt. Gregory Busch purchased this monster Shipping Board tug while in his early 20s and spent seven years rebuilding the tired old steamer from the ground up. The 150-footer was launched as the *Humaconna* in 1919 at the Superior, WI yard of the Whitney Brothers. It was repowered in 1952 with a 1500-HP Cleveland 16-258S replacing her original Filer & Stowel triple expansion steam engine. She returned to the Lakes in 1962 for Nicholson Transit and later worked for Stender before being purchased by Busch in 1977. By then the tug was overdue for another overhaul. Busch gutted the whole tug, including most of its cabin and all machinery and decks. It was completely reconstructed and repowered with a pair of 12-244 Alco locomotive engines (each 1600-HP at 900-RPMs) turning a single screw through a huge reduction gear salvaged from a Destroyer-Escort. Much of the steel used to rebuild the tug was floor plating from inside the buildings of the DeFoe shipyard, purchased at auction when the yard closed. In 1995, its starboard engine was replaced

with another 12-244, removed from a retired Michigan Limestone locomotive, of which Busch owned several. Today the tug is kept busy on the Lakes in the general towing trade, moving barge-loads of miscellaneous cargos across all five Great Lakes. The tug is pictured in 1997 outbound Marinette harbor with two loaded sand scows.

One of the more well known tugs on the Lakes is Great Lakes Dredge & Dock's big lake tug *Wm. A. Lydon*. The graceful 115-footer was built by Manitowoc Shipbuilding (Hull No. 224) in 1926. It was powered by a 900-HP Fairbanks Morse engine. The massive 6-cylinder had a 16" bore and 20" stroke. She was one of the earliest diesel-powered tugs on the Lakes. It was re-engined in 1950 with a 16-cylinder Cleveland 278A. GLD&D, her owner for sixty-six years, sold the boat to Holly Marine Towing in 1992. Unfortunately, she was renamed, becoming their *Holly Ann* and in 1996 was repowered a third time, now with a 16-567C EMD engine. *Roger LeLievre photo*

Great Lakes Towing's *Ohio* handles most of their lake work these days. The tug was built in 1903 as the City of Milwaukee's fire tug *M. F. D. No. 15*. The Towing Company is only the second owner, having picked her up in 1952. At that time the tug was converted to diesel-electric with a 16-278A Cleveland. The tug was rechristened *Lawrence C. Turner*, honoring the company's president who took office in 1946. When the tug entered service in 1954, their famous salvage and ice-breaking tug *Favorite* was decommissioned, having been virtually put out of work since the construction of USCG *Mackinaw*. In 1973 the *Turner* was renamed *Ohio*. This was probably because earlier the same year, the original Type 2 tug *Ohio* had been crushed against a Buffalo dock by a ship. Her machinery was removed for use in the *Nebraska* and the tug scrapped. In 1977, the larger *Ohio* was repowered again, this time with a 2000-HP EMD 16-645-E6 and a Falk 3.571:1 reduction gear with a slip clutch.

The tug *Evans McKeil* is moored at Port Colborne for winter lay-up in this March 2003 photo. Her tank barge *Salty Dog No. 1* is on the wall behind her. The barge would only sail one more season before being scrapped exactly across the river from where she is in this photo. International Marine Salvage went to work on it and in a matter of weeks the tanker was history. Her tug was owned by the Panama Railroad Company from the day she was launched until 1970. The PRR had it built at Balboa in 1936 under the name *Alhajuela*. The tug had a diesel electric propulsion system with its main generator spun by an Ingersoll-Rand diesel. The 110-foot tug was purchased by Keith Malcolm in 1970 and brought into the Lakes as the *Barbara Ann*. The tug has since been repowered with a 2000-HP EMD 16-645-E6 diesel. A towing machine was added inside the aft cabin and stairs to the pilothouse were cut into the forward cabin. Since being purchased by McKeil in 1989, the tug has been used to power not only the *Salty Dog* but the *McAsphalt 401* as well.

Selvick Marine Towing purchased the former Chicago fire tug *Illinois* in 1972 from Consolidated Papers who had been using it as a pulpwood rafting tug. She was built in 1898 at Chicago and powered by a 750-IHP high-pressure, non-condensing 2-cylinder steam engine. It was sold surplus in 1941 to Roen Steamship and repowered with a 1928-vintage 840-HP Fairbanks Morse diesel. They renamed the tug *John Roen III*. In 1974 the tug was named *John M. Selvick* in honor of William Selvick's son. Today, John is the owner of Marine Management and the Calumet River Fleeting Company which purchased the *John M.* for scrap in 1996. She was repowered in the late 1990s with a 1950-HP EMD 16-645. The tug is pictured in action on October 14, 2005, pushing three barge loads of heavy lift cargo on the Welland canal bound for Oswego.

MCM Marine's *William C. Gaynor* is in Cleveland picking up the big dredge *No. 55* on June 21, 2002. They purchased the tug from Lake Michigan Contractors earlier that year and restored its original name. Since 1988 it had been named *Captain Barnaby*. The 100-footer was built by DeFoe at Bay City for Great Lakes Dredge & Dock. The *No. 55* and its sister *No. 56* had also been built for GLD&D and later sold to LMC. The *Gaynor* was originally powered by an 8-cylinder 498 diesel, an engine that some of the G-tugs had experimented with. In the early 1990s though, it was repowered with a 1500-HP 12-cylinder 645 EMD.

The *Jacklyn M.* had been sitting in a Tampa, FL shipyard when the LaFarge Corporation purchased the tug to mate up with their newly constructed cement barge *Integrity*. And that's *hauling* cement, not *made* of cement. The pair entered service in 1997, a move that pretty much sealed the fate of the steamers *S. T. Crapo* and *E. M. Ford*, which have not run since. The *Jacklyn* was built by Halter in Pierre Part, LA in 1976 as the *Andrew Martin*. She originally had 7500-HP worth of Stork-Werkspoor diesels but was repowered in 1991 (after an engine room fire) with a pair of Cat 3608s. In a rare move, the Cats were actually replaced over the winter of 2001-02 and a set of 20-645 EMDs were put in their place. Normally Cats are quite reliable engines although it seems this particular tug had a set of lemons and I don't mean color-wise. In 2004, the boat was renamed *G. L. Ostrander*, in honor of Gary Ostrander, a long-time LaFarge executive who retired that March. *Wendell Wilke photo*

Andrie's tug *Karen Andrie* is mated up with barge *A-397* and loading asphalt at Marathon's Fort Street facility on the Rouge River in this June 28, 2003, image. The 120-foot tug was originally Gulfcoast Transit's *Sarah Hays*, working the coastal trade from Tampa, FL. It is powered by a pair of 16-645-E2 diesels, totaling 3600-HP. Today, regulations have mostly eliminated single screw tugs from the oil trade. Now for safety reasons, all you will see with petroleum products are these big twin screw tugs with double-hulled oil barges. The *Karen* was Hull No. 597, built at Gulfport Shipbuilding in 1965 at Port Arthur, TX. It came to the Lakes, purchased by the Muskegon-based Andrie, Inc. in 1993.

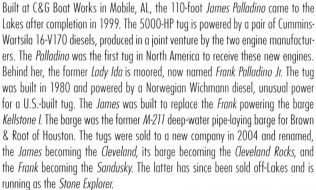

Built at C&G Boat Works in Mobile, AL, the 110-foot *James Palladino* came to the Lakes after completion in 1999. The 5000-HP tug is powered by a pair of Cummins-Wartsila 16-V170 diesels, produced in a joint venture by the two engine manufacturers. The *Palladino* was the first tug in North America to receive these new engines. Behind her, the former *Lady Ida* is moored, now named *Frank Palladino Jr.* The tug was built in 1980 and powered by a Norwegian Wichmann diesel, unusual power for a U.S.-built tug. The *James* was built to replace the *Frank* powering the barge *Kellstone I.* The barge was the former *M-211* deep-water pipe-laying barge for Brown & Root of Houston. The tugs were sold to a new company in 2004 and renamed, the *James* becoming the *Cleveland,* its barge becoming the *Cleveland Rocks,* and the *Frank* becoming the *Sandusky.* The latter has since been sold off-Lakes and is running as the *Stone Explorer.*

In this January 2002 photo, the *Susan W. Hannah* is locked into the notch of the self-unloading cement barge *Southdown Conquest.* The 1977 tug was built in Mississippi for the off-shore Gulf trade until coming to the Lakes for Hannah in 1986. She is powered by a pair of 12-clyinder EMD 645s. The barge was converted from the 1937 Amoco tanker *Red Crown.* It has since been bought by St. Mary's Cement and renamed *St. Mary's Conquest.* In addition to this barge, the steamships *St. Marys Challenger* and *CTC No. 1* are all managed by Hannah Marine out of Chicago.

In 1928, Great Lakes Dredge & Dock ordered a new 125-foot lake tug from Manitowoc Shipbuilding. Like the others designed for GLD&D, she was ahead of her time. Diesel powered and outfitted with the most sophisticated navigational equipment, the tug was launched in 1928 as the *John F. Cushing*. Later it was renamed *Olive M. Moore* for the Socony Oil Company. The tug's Busch-Sulzer 1000-HP diesel was replaced in 1968 with a Fairbanks Morse 10-38D-8-1/8 2000-HP engine. The long, sleek, low-profile tug was reconstructed with an upper pilothouse. It was sold to Escanaba interests in 1969 and received another reconstruction. It was mated up with the old craneship *Buckeye*, which had been converted to a barge. In 1980, after a conversion to twin screw, the tug received a pair of 3000-HP turbocharged Alco diesels. The tug was reconstructed for a fourth time and years later a fifth time, each one taking the tug further and further from its original appearance. Over the winter of 2005-2006, the tug was rebuilt again at the Erie shipyard and was mated up with the former Oglebay Norton steamer *Buckeye*, which had just received a barge conversion. Today,

the giant tug shows no signs what-so-ever of her 1928 construction. Even her hull plates are new. It would be interesting to learn what, if anything, is actually left from the Manitowoc construction. An interesting fact is that the *Moore* has been the power-plant for *both* former Columbia steamships named *Buckeye* that were later converted to barges. *Wendell Wilke photo*

The 150-foot tug *Joseph H. Thompson Jr.* was built from remains of the stern section of the steamer *Joseph H. Thompson*. The bow and cargo section of this old steamship were converted to a barge by the same name and today the pair are mated up as a tug-barge unit. The tug was built in the late 1980s and entered service in 1990 for Upper Lakes Towing. The composite unit can be found in action all over the Lakes, carrying everything from taconite to salt.

Originally, the *Joe Thompson Jr.* was powered by three 25-ton General Electric diesels. The 16-cylinder model 7FDM medium speed engines produce a total of 9,000-HP. The 7FDM engine was used in locomotives as well and comes in 8-, 12-, and 16-cylinder models. It is still made today and is becoming a popular choice in marine applications. The engine is a 4-stroke turbocharged engine that measures nearly 18-feet long. The three engines supplied power to a single gigantic Falk gearbox from a belt-driven electric propulsion system. In 2006, the tug received a major overhaul at the shipyard in Erie and was refitted with a pair of Caterpillar diesels.

The tug *Alice A.* is pictured in dry dock at Heddle Marine in Hamilton during March 2002. It is undergoing a rebuild as an ATB unit with the barge *McCleary's Spirit*. Sitting behind her, the bright orange bow of that barge is visible. Also protruding from her pilothouse roof is a large circular base which will soon hold an upper wheelhouse needed for visibility over the barge. It will lock into the barge using a Bludworth coupling system. She offers 60-tons of bollard pull and is powered by a pair of 16-cylinder EMDs. The 4400-hp coastal tug measures 135' x 34' x 18' and was built as the *Raider IV*. It was completed in 1970 at the Adelaide Ship Construction yard in Australia. Now sailing as the *William J. Moore*, the tug is in service on the Great Lakes. *Jason R. LaDue photo*

The *Esther Moran* is caught in action at Norfolk in September 1998. The tug was sold Canadian in 2000, becoming McKeil's *Salvor*. She was built in 1963 at Oyster Bay, NY (Jakobson Shipyard, Hull No. 417) for Moran Towing of New York City. The tug was brought into the Lakes via the St. Lawrence Seaway in 2000 and in June was placed on the blocks at Heddle's Drydock in Hamilton for an overhaul. The tug was built with an electric propulsion system. Two 16-cylinder 278A Cleveland diesels were turning Allis-Chalmers generators, supplying power to Westinghouse propulsion motors. Since then, the twin screw tug has been repowered with 16-cylinder EMD 645s. *Robert J. Lewis photo*

Resting in the Purvis Marine yard at Sault Ste. Marie, Ontario, is their giant tug *Anglian Lady*. The boat was built in Southampton, England in 1953 by the J. I. Thornycroft Company. The ocean-going tug was originally named *Hamtun* and operated by the Southampton, Isle of Wight & South England Royal Mail Steam Packet Company. Purvis bought the tug in 1989 but it had already been given its present name a year earlier, while still in British registry. She is powered by a pair of 12-cylinder German Deutz diesels.

It's March 1999 and the Lakes' newest tug *Dorothy Ann* is receiving the finishing touches in Escanaba. Soon she will power the new self-unloading barge *Pathfinder*, built off the hull of the old steamer *J. L. Mauthe*. Alongside her in this image is fleetmate *Joyce L. Van Enkevort* which powered the *Mauthe* in its first year of operation until its own barge was completed. Today the *Joyce* is mated with the *Great Lakes Trader*. These huge tugs are built with tremendous power and are tall enough to see well over the 700-foot barges they are married to. The *Dorothy* was built at Bay Shipbuilding (Hull No. 743) but completed at Escanaba by Van Enkevort. The 119-footer is built to ABS standards and measures in at 1,090 gross tons. She is powered by twin 20-cylinder EMD 645-E7B diesels with Z-drive propulsion units. The two EMDs produce a total of 7,200-HP.

Pere Marquette Shipping's *Undaunted* rests at its home port of Ludington, MI during winter lay-up. The former Navy ATA was refitted in 1998 as the notch tug for the barge *Pere Marquette 41*. Her structural modifications and widening are obvious in this photo. The tug was ordered by the U.S. Navy as an Ocean Rescue Tug, intended to be named *ATR-126*. However, plans changed and the tug was completed in 1944 as the Auxiliary Fleet Tug *ATA-199*. The tug was decommissioned shortly after the war and by 1948 was in a Maritime Commission reserve fleet. That year, the *ATA*s were redesignated and the *199* became the *ATA-199 Undaunted*, a name she would never see service under. In 1963 the 143-footer was transferred to the Kings Point Merchant Marine Academy and used as a training vessel under the name *Kings Point*.

The *Kings Point* was purchased by Basic Towing in 1993 and brought into the Lakes. It sat idle at Escanaba until a sale to Pere Marquette. The boat was refit at the Basic Marine shipyard. A new, much taller pilothouse was constructed and the tug widened for installation of a Bark River pin system designed by Clyde Van Enkevort. In this photo, massive pins extend out through the tug's hull and lock themselves into the notch of their barge. They are hydraulically operated. In 1998, the tug re-entered service under its old name *Undaunted* and currently powers the 5600-ton capacity barge *Pere Marquette 41*.

The *Undaunted* is powered by a pair of beautifully maintained 12-278A Cleveland diesels. General Motors displayed their first 2-stroke V-12 diesel at the 1933 World's Fair and the same year the U.S. Navy announced its intentions to dieselize its entire fleet. General Motors became a major supplier of marine-use diesel engines for ship propulsion systems. The bulk of the tugboats from the WW-II era received either the Cleveland 278A or EMD 567A engine, both 1200-HP V-12 General Motors products. The ex-Navy ocean-going tug *Undaunted* is a single screw boat with two 12-278A diesels turning generators that supply power for twin propulsion motors feeding a huge single gearbox. A diesel-electric set-up similar to this (with a four-pack of 16-cylinder Cleveland 278As) was the primary source of propulsion in submarines for the U.S. Navy during WW-II.

The comfortable lake tug *W. N. Twolan* began life in 1962. She was built by Davie at Lauzon, Quebec, for the government of Canada, National Harbours Board. It served as a harbor tug at Churchill, Manitoba until 1986. At that time, McKeil Marine of Hamilton purchased her and brought the tug into the Lakes where she was used for general towing duties.

In 1995, the *W. N. Twolan* was purchased by Buchannan Forest Products of Thunder Bay. It is operated by ABM Marine and mated up with the lumber barge *McAllister 132*. The tug is powered by two direct reversing Stork-Werkspoor diesels. Originating in the Netherlands, the model TMAS-278, 8-cylinder turbocharged diesels produce 1600-HP.

The burned-out hulk of the tug *Vortice* is pictured at McKeil's Hamilton yard on March 17, 1997. The tug has seen some action in its short career. It was built in 1976 at Mangone Shipbuilding in Houston, TX for a Norwegian operator. Named *Musketeer Fury*, the tug was placed in ocean service, powered by a pair of EMD diesels. It went through a series of names for Norwegian and Italian owners until 1993 when a fire left the tug stranded southwest of the Azores in the Atlantic Ocean. It was towed into Treiste, Italy on August 26, 1993, and laid-up. Finally in 1996, McKeil Marine bought the tug and brought it into the Lakes via the St. Lawrence Seaway system.

In December 1998, the *Vortice* left under tow bound for Norfolk, VA. McKeil sold the tug to Sea Force Marine who intended to rebuild the tug and have it operated by Bay Gulf Trading. A small fortune was invested in the reconstruction of this 150-foot tug. It was renamed *Norfolk* but sat at the shipyard without any action. Occasionally, you'd see some smoke coming out of her stacks but the tug never seemed to see any service. In 2005, the tug was towed back into the Lakes, delivered to Bay Ship where all the bugs were worked out, modifications were made, and she was prepared for service in the cement trade. Her purchaser, LaFarge North America, used the tug to mate up with their newly constructed barge *Innovation*, as an ATB unit. The tug was renamed and entered service as the *Samuel de Champlain*. As the *Norfolk*, the tug is pictured at a Norfolk shipyard on November 11, 2003.

ABM's twin-screw *Radium Yellowknife* is powered by a pair of 850-HP V-12 Caterpillar D398 diesels. The starboard engine pictured here has been named *Pricilla* by her loving engineers. The name and a smiling face are visible on her air intake. I'm sure the port side engine, *Pricilla's* sister, also has a name. The Caterpillar D379 (V-8), D398 (V-12) and the D399 (V-16) have been around for a long time now and are starting to become "classics." Parts are still plentiful though and these engines are a common source of power for tugboats.

Eastbound on the Welland Canal is the *Petite Forte* shoving the barge *St. Marys Cement*. The tug dates back to 1969, quite new for a boat on the Great Lakes. It was built by Cochrane & Sons in Selby, England and went into Panamanian registry upon completion. For her first two years, the tug was named *E. Bronson Ingram,* a name which soon changed to *Jaramac 42.* United Towing bought the tug in 1973 and brought her into British registry as the *Scotsman.* This tug has truly been around the world and in 1981 her life took another drastic change. She was sold to Arabian Bulk Trade Limited and renamed *Al Battal* under Saudi Arabian registry. In 1986 the tug came to the Great Lakes to work the cement trade. At that time she was given her present name and has been in action here ever since. The tug is powered by two 8-cylinder, English-built, Ruston diesels.

On May 11, 2004, the self-unloading cement barge *St. Marys Cement II* is offloading into the hopper of a storage facility in Cleveland. The barge was built in 1978 as the *Velasco.* In her notch is the tug *Sea Eagle II,* built in 1979 by Modern Marine in Houma, LA. The tug was originally named *Sea Eagle* under U.S. flag but the "*II*" was added in 1991, numbering the tug as Canadians love to do. It is powered by two 20-645-E7 turbocharged diesels, producing 7200-HP. St. Mary's Cement Corporation has owned the tug and barge since 1991.

McKeil's new grey and orange paint scheme has just been applied to their big ocean tug *John Spence*. She is downbound the St. Clair River pushing a loaded asphalt barge. The tug was built as an off-shore supply vessel (OSV) for Federal Commerce & Navigation. It was constructed in 1972 as the *Mary B. VI* at the Star Shipyard in New Westminister, BC. The tug is powered by a pair of 1600-HP 16-567C EMDs.

The *John Spence* was given her current name in 1994. McKeil had purchased the tug the year before from the Artic Transportation Company, who had been running her as the *Artic Tuktu* since 1983. In this image she is nestled in for lay-up at Sarnia. Surrounding her are several big self-unloading freighters, all sitting silent for winter while their crews are busy inside making repairs for another busy season on the Lakes.

This series of 40-foot dredge tenders owned by the Canal Corporation could easily have been placed in the "Small Tugs" chapter but they were built for a specific service on the Erie Canal. They've been on the canal their entire lives—all ten of these nearly identical tugs. In this photo, the *Tender 1* is moored alongside a barge at "Mud Lock" (Lock 1) of the Cayuga-Seneca Canal on June 20, 2002.

Chapter 8
Canal Tugs

An unusual breed of tugs can be found scattered up and down the East Coast and on the Great Lakes. A connecting link between these two geographical regions is the New York State Barge Canal, otherwise known as "The Erie Canal." It is a man-made waterway; a system of locks, twists and turns, quaint small towns, shallow water, low bridges and scenery that provides an indescribable beauty for those lucky enough to make the transit.

Eastbound through the middle of New York State, at Three Rivers Junction, the canal splits and you can continue on towards Buffalo, exiting the west end at Tonawanda. Or you can head up the Oswego River on a leg of the canal that spills out at Oswego. From Waterford to Oswego the air-draft restriction is 20-feet. From Three Rivers to Tonawanda it is 15-feet. Today, the western portion is in desperate need of dredging so nearly all commercial traffic is forced to exit at Oswego, cross Lake Ontario, and transit the Welland Canal (bypassing Niagara Falls) if their destination is Lake Erie or points west.

On the east end, this canal begins at Waterford, a small town above Troy, NY on the west side of the Hudson River. Picture it: You're running a tugboat, pushing an oil barge. Heading up the Hudson, past Troy, you transit the Federal Lock and pass the famous John E. Matton shipyard on your left. Nearing Waterford, you spot a big green street sign-like message marking the Erie Canal "that way ⇨." You hang a left and pass the museum ship *Day Peckinpaugh* and canal tug *Chancellor* and right there, the first low bridge is staring right at you. And I mean *low.*

This is where most big powerful tugboats might as well just turn around. However, the early canal tugs were built with special low-profile pilothouses, enabling them to run the Erie Canal and duck under all these bridges.

These first canallers, some of which still exist, were powerful and built for ocean service in addition to their harbor and canal duties. These tugs would push barges, often times heavily loaded with oil, up and down the Erie Canal, delivering their products to and from the East Coast.

These canal tugs, or "canallers" as they've come to be known, were employed in harbor and ocean service in the winter months when the canal closed. Sometimes a temporary upper pilothouse was added, providing visibility for the skipper. In the 1940s a retractable pilothouse was experimented with and by the 1950s, this was a standard feature on most canallers. The pilothouse would be mounted on a large air or hydraulic ram, much like a car hoist at your local automotive shop. The whole pilothouse could be raised up and down—up to see over a high cargo or tall empty barge and down to duck under those pesky low bridges.

As cargo trends shifted with the times, commercial traffic was reduced and today very few operators remain active on the canal. The New York State Marine Highway Transportation Company is probably *the* canal operator of today, with their big canaller *Margot* and the Gladding-Hearn-built *Benjamin Elliot.* In addition to regular cargos of heavy-lift machinery, this firm is chosen several times throughout each year to tow unusual vessels or loads through the system. The canal also sees its fair share of vessels coming or going from the Lakes, after being purchased or sold. Often times it is interesting to watch owners attempt to make the transit with a boat *way* too big for the canal. Special ballasting needs to take place and often their height needs to be modified with a "gas ax," torching off all the masts and sometimes even the smokestacks, or the top portion, anyway.

Aside from a few independent tugboat companies running the canal, a large fleet of tugboats can be found in service, owned by the New York State

Tender 4 and the tug *Erie* are stationed along the Erie Canal. The state tugs are known for their old-fashioned rope fenders. Building this fendering is truly a lost art in tugboating today. The *Tender 4,* like all in this series, was built in 1928 by American Boiler Works at Erie, PA. They are very similar and were perhaps the inspiration for the Oatka-class tugs built at Marine Iron a decade later.

"Just hangin' out." On April 20, 2001, the *Tender 8* leans against a post in the Lyons dry-dock. She is waiting for a crew to fetch her for another season of work on the canal, which will be opening in a couple weeks. In the background, up on the hill, the old derrick boat *DB-2A* is in long-term lay-up.

At Waterford in November 2005, the state tug *Urger* is about ready for winter lay-up. The beautifully maintained tug dates back to 1901, built by Johnston Brothers at Ferrysburg as the fish tug *H. J. Dornbos.* It worked for the Ver Duin Brothers of Grand Haven until 1922 when it was sold to the State of New York, Department of Transportation for $22,000. The steam tug was then converted to a towing vessel. It became the flagship of the Canal Corporation in the 1990s and each season can be found keeping busy throughout the canal system.

At Baldwinsville, NY, the Canal Corporation's tug *Seneca* is docked for the weekend in this April 2001 photo. Built in 1932, the beautiful 65-foot tug is similar in design and appearance to many Corps of Engineers tugs of the same size. Coincidently, tugboats named *Seneca* exist in service on the Great Lakes, Erie Canal, and both the West and East Coasts.

Canal Corporation. These famous blue and yellow tugs are known to be beautifully maintained with their polished brass, woodwork and old-fashioned rope fendering. They operate a fleet of dredges and other equipment needed to maintain the waterway.

While traffic has dwindled on the Erie Canal, today many of these specialized tugs still exist. Many of them have had their pilothouses welded firm in the "up" position, since they no longer need to be functional. Other times, their retractable houses are removed altogether and given a more traditional look.

In their early years, many two-deck harbor tugs had been modified as canallers. Their upper pilothouse, railings, stack and other fittings were cut off and a retractable house built in its place. The forward portion of the main deckhouse, under the pilothouse, needed to be gutted with a new bulkhead and ram installed. These rams are found below deck extending up through the main deck into the cabin and attached to the lower framing of the pilothouse. These pilothouses are usually quite short in length, as to not take up much cabin space down below.

This "void" in the main cabin provides a space for the house to slide down into when lowered. Under the house, connected to both floors is some sort of folding guide to keep all the piping and wiring in order. In this application, wiring and piping must all be in the form of heavy duty rubber hosing and other materials that can stand decades of bending as the house is raised and lowered.

Another place these canallers still have value is in the port of Chicago and its connecting waterways. Chicago is home to the same low bridges that require a low air-draft to pass under. Dozens of tugs in that vicinity can be found today that were built as canallers. Even modern towboats in the area have retractable houses. These flat-front river boats are used to push large tows of multiple barges from down river points such as Lemont or Joliet up to South Chicago on the Calumet River. These canal-style towboats take the big river tows, split them up, sort out the barges, and move the appropriate ones up towards the Lake. There, local tugboat companies such as Calumet River Fleeting, Holly Marine Towing, and Kindra Lake Towing, will fleet these barges and move them to and from their ultimate destinations. "Fleeting" is a term applied to the temporary mooring of a particular barge. These tug companies, using canal tugs, will shuffle these barges around in their "fleet" and, going by the ever-changing orders from the office, will make sure each barge gets to where it is going at the right time and date.

From South Chicago these canallers will push or tow the barges, usually several at once, across to Indiana Harbor, Gary, or Burns Harbor, serving the mills. Much of it is scrap going to or steel coils coming from the steel mills. Calumet River Fleeting and Holly Marine also have runs further north, towing large barges able to handle more severe weather in the open water. Cargos up towards Holland on the Michigan side and to Manitowoc on the Wisconsin side are a common sight.

Seneca is powered by two 240-HP Cummins diesels driving electric generators that power two G.E. propulsion motors run through a common gearbox, applying all her power to a single screw. It is one of the smallest tugs around with a diesel-electric propulsion system. Here, an open inspection cover reveals well adjusted brushes and a spotless commutator, the signs of a hard-working crew that actually cares about their tug. In today's world of crewing cutbacks and limited budgets, preventive maintenance often becomes overlooked.

Showing her crew's pride, the Seneca's skipper keeps her brass polished and woodwork gleaming. The classic tug has won many awards at the tugboat gatherings and the plaques are proudly displayed on the back wall, including the "Scariest Looking Crew" award. In this image, her throttle stands display the "General Electric" logo, giving away what's "under the hood." A brass whistle pull hangs down in front of the beautiful woodwork of her two-piece drop-down windows.

At Sylvan Beach on the east end of Oneida Lake, the tug *Governor Roosevelt* is employed on a dredging job in this October 9, 2005, photo. The 75-foot tug was built at Buffalo as a low-profile canal tug in 1928. She and her sister, *Governor Cleveland*, were built for the Buffalo Marine Construction Corporation but transferred to the State of New York after only a couple years. They were originally steam but have both since been converted to diesel.

The state tug *Reliable* is pictured above Lock E-16 on the Erie Canal. Its Atlas-Imperial engine has been removed and the tug awaits her fate. The 74-foot tug was built in Syracuse in 1934 along with its twin sister *Syracuse*, which is still in service. The *Reliable's* engine is one serial number off from the identical engine powering their tug *Urger*. The engine is in Waterford, now as a parts source for the *Urger*.

Above the locks at Waterford, the historic old tug *Buffalo* is undergoing a rebuild. The stout little tug has been a staple on the barge canal for many decades. Heavy-duty rubrails and rope fendering stand out against her blue and yellow hull. The cabin roof has been removed for engine room surgery. Every inch of the proud old tug is being rebuilt as part of a local restoration effort.

The folks are doing an excellent job on the *Buffalo*. New woodwork throughout the entire pilothouse is shiny, probably looking better than the day she was built. Her front windows are of an unusual arrangement with some rather large blind spots. The museum tug is now owned by the town of Waterford.

Down below is a Cooper Bessemer model GN6 diesel. The direct drive engine produces 200-HP at 300-RPM. It has a 10-1/2-inch stroke and a 13-1/2-inch bore. In this photo, her engineers are studying the project, discussing the next steps. The engine is receiving a complete rebuild. Her block is exposed with the heads gone and liners pulled out. Duct tape is carefully placed over areas where dust and debris are not well received in an operational engine.

Up on the dock, the *Buffalo's* engine is spread out in pieces. Her cylinder liners and heads rest on stands to be worked on. Here, three liners are uncovered, posing for a photo while their "home" (the tug) sits in the background, waiting patiently for the day she will again be able to run.

A westbound canal tug approaches lock E-17 which is open and ready with a green light giving the "come-on-in" signal. A unique feature of this lock is the concrete "wall" you pass under with a gate that drops down to close the lock. Typically locks have doors that swing open and closed. However, E-17 has the highest lift of the system and is designed quite differently. While some locks have a lift as little as a few feet, E-17 raises you more than 40-feet up to the "downtown" of Little Falls, NY. The passage through this town is extremely scenic by boat. The highway and railway bridges and openings such as this lock entrance look mighty low from an approaching tug! As captain, it's easy to subconsciously "duck" while maneuvering under these tight spots, waiting to hear or feel the bridge rip the top of your pilothouse off. Sometimes clearance is literally just an inch or two.

At a tall lock on the Oswego River, a large canal tug is heading north, bound for Lake Ontario. The tug is all the way into the lock, up tight to the doors, making room for its tow that barely fit behind them. Once the boat or boats are into the lock, they'll hold their position while the control valves are opened and the water is slowly dumped out of the lock, lowering the vessels until they are even with the water level below. At that point, the doors are swung open and the tug is given the green light to exit the lock. In this image, the view from the tug's pilothouse is directly into the side of a highway bridge that just happens to pass right over the lock. When the lock is lowered, they will pass under the bridge. The locks are controlled from the little booth to the left.

The tug *Chancellor* has her jack-up house in the lowered position in this photo at Kingston, NY on March 15, 2003. The tug was built with a fixed low house and dual smoke stacks. She was launched in 1938 at Brooklyn, having been built at the Ira Bushey yard. The name changed to *James J. Kehoe* in 1962 and was last operated by the Kosnac family in NYC before returning to the canal. It was then run by the McHughs, in service on the Erie Canal. Her original name was restored in 1990 when the tug went for museum use.

Chancellor is powered by a rare Fairbanks, Morse & Company diesel engine. Today the tug is on display below the Waterford Lock E-2 but can still be found in action at the popular annual Tugboat Roundup. It is owned and operated by the Waterford Historical Society.

The John E. Matton & Sons shipyard was a well-known tugboat builder. They built a number of canal-style tugs, many for their own use, at their yard near the Erie Canal at Cohoes, NY. The *Athena*, originally named *John E. Matton*, was built in 1939 with a low pilothouse. Years later it was plated over and a fixed upper house constructed. At that time, her smokestack was also raised. A stepped-down cabin is usually a give-away of Matton construction. Her gold stripe cuts a "Z" near that cabin change, appropriate for the tugs owner, the Zenith Tugboat Company. Another interesting observation about the *Athena* is she has two runs of wooden rub-rails from bow to stern. Plenty of bow fendering has been added and facing wires hang loosely over the side that lead through a roller chock and double back to her winches on the bow. These are used for facing-up to barges when pushing. *Nick Silva photo*

The *Athena* was originally powered by a 6-cylinder Winton engine. In 1958 it was repowered by a beautiful 8-cylinder 567C EMD engine. Its gearbox, pictured here, is a 2.518:1 ratio Falk 10MB. Falk began making marine drive gears in 1916, the first having gone into a WW-I submarine. Since then they became one of the big names in marine transmissions, commonly found mated up with big tug engines such as Cleveland, EMD, and Fairbanks Morse. On the left in the photo is her clutch; on the right, her propeller shaft leads into a carrier bearing.

On the side of *Athena's* 567 engine is her starter. The tug's engines are either started electrically (requiring tremendous battery power, normally a dozen or so locomotive batteries fed by a battery charger run off the auxiliary generator) or in this case, by air. An air starter such as this bolts firmly to the engine block. High pressure air is sent to the starter which, through a reduction gear of its own, applies tremendous power to the engine's ring gear, turning the engine over for a start. When the engine seems to be firing off, the engineer will release the starter valve and the spring-loaded bendix kicks out. They are tuned precisely to line up for a tight fit, the gear head on the bendix to the flywheel. This can be seen on the left end in this image. On the right end is an air supply line (underneath, leading in) and out the back is a vent for the discharged air. Ninety-degree pipe fittings aim that vent towards the bilge, because when you start one of these things they blow a huge volume of air, oil and condensation which is best left down below rather than in the engineers face.

Old friends, stopping to chat. At the Junction Lock on October 8, 2005, the canallers *Margot* and *Sharon Elizabeth* have pulled over for a quick visit, each tug having been traveling in the opposite direction. The *Sharon* is on her delivery trip into the Lakes, bound for Zenith Tug's yard in Duluth. The *Margot* is owned by the New York State Marine Highway Transportation Company and was heading eastbound with the barge *Lockwood 1000*. The pair had been transporting heavy-lift cargos of turbines this season. In this photo, the tug poses with her pilothouse in the raised position.

Again she poses, this time with the house in the lowered position. The hydraulic pilothouses came into play in the 1950s, at which time nearly all of the fixed low houses were replaced with this up and down type. The *Margot* was built in 1958 at the Jakobson Shipyard in Oyster Bay. She was originally Moran's *Margot Moran* and built as a canaller. Before returning to the canal trade in 2004, the *Margot* wore the highly visible orange and black colors of the Kosnac Floating Derrick Corporation of New York City.

The *Margot's* main engine is an 8-cylinder Fairbanks Morse 38D8-1/8 diesel. This is an opposed piston diesel, which, as you can see in the photo, really has no heads. There are two pistons in each cylinder compressing against each other with an upper and lower crankshaft. They tend to be complicated engines when it comes time for repair but are quite reliable and offer tremendous horsepower. These "O/Ps" as the engineers know them, became quite popular in the tugboats. It's obvious in this photo that the *Margot's* engine room is kept in immaculate condition.

Zenith's *Sharon Elizabeth* is moored at Troy, NY on the Hudson River, awaiting prep work to be completed on her tow which, as is, was too high to transit the canal from that point onward. The tug was built in 1938 at DeFoe Boat & Motor Works in Bay City, MI. She was designed for the U.S. Navy and built as a "test unit" along with a nearly identical sister. In cooperation with Moran Towing, General Electric and General Motors, the tug was built, tests were conducted and the end result was an extremely successful design. Upon completion of Naval testing, the tug was delivered to Moran Towing who had funded its construction and had her built with a canal house. Soon after, the Navy began an ambitious construction program, cranking out hundreds of these "ultimate harbor tugs," which they designated "YTB" (Yard Tug – Big). The *Sharon*, built as the *Thomas E. Moran*, and her sister tug *William J. Moran* were Hulls No. 161 and 162 at DeFoe. They were the prototypes for the Navy's famous WWII-era YTB tugs.

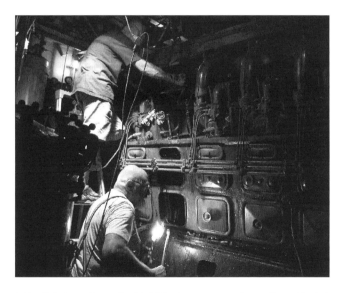

In New York City on September 24, 2005, the engineers on the tug *Sharon Elizabeth* have a cylinder pulled out for replacement. The giant Cleveland 12-278A diesel turns a generator creating electricity to power her dual propulsion motors. While approaching New York, the tug's chief engineer reported a water leak somewhere in the engine. The tug was stopped in order to make repairs and upon closer inspection, a liner was found to be cracked. The liners sit down in the block on an O-ring and if that seal goes out, cooling water can leak directly into the lube oil, eventually diluting it to the point of destroying the engine. This can happen very quickly and with little notice. They say good help is hard to find but the chief's watchful eye that day probably saved this engine's life.

The *Statesboro* is ready for action in this nighttime photo in New York City. She is moored at her former owner's dock on Staten Island, awaiting the next leg of her journey up the Hudson River bound for the Great Lakes. After her Moran days, the tug continued to work in the New York City area as the *Viking*. In 1993 it was purchased by Capt. Norman Assey Jr. and brought to Georgetown, SC. This was the first tug for his new company, Georgetown Towing. The firm is still in operation today, owned by McAllister Towing. In addition to the interesting fact about the tug being the prototype for the YTB, during WW-II it was requisitioned by the Navy for wartime service. It was actually assigned a YTB number, becoming the Navy's *USS Namontack YTB-738* for the duration of the war. Moran bought the tug back in 1947. In the extreme low position, her pilothouse would be completely buried in its lower cabin and the skipper would need to look through the windows through the portholes below. Very limited visibility! In addition to going lower, the house will raise up another four feet from the position in this photo.

The tug's old-fashioned clinometer has long ago been stolen so a crewmember has used a Sharpie to fill in the lines of the old one. As the days turn into weeks at sea, this type of creativity tends to show up mysteriously throughout the tug. The *Statesboro*, formerly the *Sharon Elizabeth*, has a monster 6:1 Farrel-Birmingham gearbox that feeds a single shaft but is powered by dual 250-Volt, 1600-Amp General Electric propulsion motors. This artwork happens to have been applied to the blower ducts pulling fresh air into the engine room above those motors.

In the Genesee River at Rochester, the canaller *Cheyenne II* is laid-up along with an old barge. The 75-foot tug was built in 1941 by Ira Bushey at Brooklyn. In mid-December 2000, oil was reported on the water south of the Stutson Street bridge. The Coast Guard investigated and found nothing. Eventually someone noted there used to be a tugboat parked there. Sure enough, divers found the old *Cheyenne II* submerged in 20-feet of water and its bilge-load of dirty oil had floated out of her. To this day the blue and white tug remains sunk in that same position. *Jason R. LaDue photo*

The *Nicole S.* is in the drydock at South Chicago for repair. John Selvick purchased the tug from Reinauer in 1986 and brought it in from Boston. While westbound on Lake Erie, the tug's EMD engine blew and they had to be towed in to Detroit. The engine was found to be a total loss and the boat was resold to Ferriss Marine Contracting. Ferriss had the old City-Class G-tug *Detroit* which was undergoing a reconstruction at their yard on the Rouge River. The newly arrived canaller *Evening Star* became priority and the *Detroit's* 12-567A EMD engine went into the *Star* instead (replacing an identical engine). After eight years of working for Ferriss under the name *Protector*, the former *Star* was resold to Selvick and is now in Chicago as the *Nicole S.*, honoring the owner's daughter. It was built in 1949 at Alexander and is a twin hull to the Gaelic tugs discussed in chapter two.

Lying in the Perth Amboy Anchorage behind Staten Island in November 2005, are two former Mobile Oil tugs, the *Tenacious* and *Dorothy Elizabeth*. They were once named *Mobile 8* and *Mobile 11*. The *Tenacious* was one of the biggest canallers ever and also one of the last ones built. It was launched in 1960 at Ingalls Shipbuilding in Pascagoula, MS. In this photo, they have tied off to say "hello" to their former fleetmate who was at anchor between jobs. The *Tenacious* is on her way to new owners on Lake Huron. The tug had worked in the New York City area and most recently out of Philly for Clearwater Marine before being sold to Ryba Marine Contracting on the Great Lakes.

The *Tenacious* is a comfortable boat. Here crewmembers enjoy pork chop night in her galley which is below deck, behind the gyro room and ahead of the engine room. These submarine galleys are not that common on the tugs. There are pros and cons. The cooking smells float right up into the quarters, but on the other hand, below the waterline it is always nice and cool, making for a decent place to hang out. Her wide cabin allows ample interior space which pays off in the crew quarters, where six guys can each have their own room. The pilothouse also is quite large, almost twice the size of your average canaller. The *Tenacious* is powered by a 1750-HP 16-567C EMD diesel. The tug has proved favorably in the construction trade on the Lakes and has already gained a reputation as a strong and fast puller.

The small canaller *Mohawk* is pictured on the Welland Canal on December 22, 1986. The tug was built in 1943 at City Island, NY for the U.S. Navy as *YTL-440*. YTL is a standard Navy designation, YT meaning "yard tug" and L meaning "little" (yes, they had medium and big sizes too). The 64-footer became a full-time Great Lakes tug when purchased by Lake Michigan Contractors in the 1990s. MCM Marine bought the tug in 2001 and is operating her today as a construction tug, doing everything from dredge tending to lake towing. *Jimmy Sprunt photo*

In 1975 the *YTL-440* was sold into civilian hands and converted to a canaller with the addition of this retractable pilothouse. The image shows exactly what goes on under the house. A big ram lifts the house up when the captain pulls the lever. Guides can be seen on the bulkhead to keep the house straight and lifting smoothly. A bundle of wire and hose is made to flex with the movement, supplying power and other essentials to the wheelhouse.

The *Donald C. Hannah* has her pilothouse dropped to duck under a low Chicago bridge. The twin screw tug was built in 1962 by Main Iron Works at Houma, LA. It is powered by a pair of 12-567C EMD engines with Falk 2.5:1 reduction gears. In 2000 the starboard engine was replaced with a 12-645 EMD. Similar engine; heavier block. The 645 hit the market in the early 1960s and for decades was *the* power for General Motors locomotives.

Heading across the lake bound for Indiana Harbor, in this November 2002 photo, is Hannah's *Hannah D. Hannah*. Whew, that's a lot of Hannahs! The tug is pushing a pair of loaded coal barges from South Chicago. Her retractable house is in a comfortable mid position. It will go either up or down, roughly another four feet. The tug was built by Sturgeon Bay Shipbuilding as Hull No. 241 in 1956. It was originally named *Harbor Ace* and designed for service in Chicago.

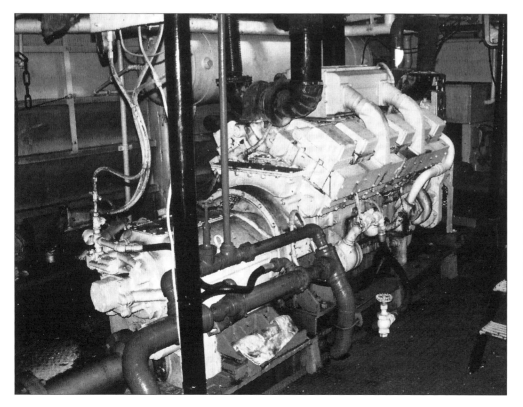

The twin screw *Hannah D. Hannah* is powered by a pair of KT-2300 Cummins diesels producing 1400-HP. The engines are turning two 4-blade Kahlenberg 60" x 54" wheels through Twin Disc 5.17:1 MG-527 gearboxes. The local tugboat companies are kept busy shuttling barges to and from the ports of Burns Harbor, Indiana Harbor, and the friendly Gary, Indiana, on the bottom of Lake Michigan. Most of the products are coming from or bound for the river system leading into the Chicago area. This makes it quite the "hot spot" for tugboat action.

At Selvick's dock in Chicago, their tug *Sea Wolf* is in for repairs as crews install new bow fendering. Its pilothouse is in its lowered position. In 2001 the tug was named *Jimmy Wray*, in honor of the company's port captain. The unusual looking tug was built in 1954 at Pascagoula, MS. It had been brought in to the Lakes from the New York City area upon purchase by the original Calumet River Fleeting Company. The twin screw tug is powered by a pair of Detroit 12V-71 diesels. A retractable pilothouse was added later.

The tug *Orion* was captured in action on August 31, 2001, at Richmond, CA. Her retractable pilothouse is in the raised position and the tug is heading out to take on another job. A large towing machine has been added to her stern. On the upper deck a small "phone booth" operator shack has been constructed, housing the aft controls. The *Orion* is now owned by Cross Link, Inc. of San Francisco but was actually Ed Barnaby's Chicago canaller *Lenny B*, named in honor of his wife. In 1976 when Barnaby repowered the tug, he also converted it to a canaller with the installation of a new retractable pilothouse. *George R. Schneider photo*

Today the *Orion's* old pilothouse sits as a shack at the old Barnaby yard below the Skyway in South Chicago. The tug was built in 1945 for the U.S. Navy as the *USS Quileute YTB-540*. Like all of the tugs of this style, she had a pair of 6-278A Clevelands powering generators to provide DC power for two large propulsion motors feeding a 6:1 Farrel-Birmingham gear. Barnaby purchased the tug in 1974 but it was found to be inoperable (propulsion motors were shot). He had the tug repowered and converted to twin screw. The new engines were a pair of brand new 1500-HP EMD 12-645-E6 diesels. The stern had to be rebuilt to accommodate the changes in propulsion. Keel coolers were also added. Her original pilothouse was unbolted from the tug during a canal transit into the Lakes.

The canaller *Waverly* was built in 1956 by the Parker Brothers Shipyard at Houston for the Sioux City & New Orleans Barge Line. It was powered by a pair of 6-278A Clevelands. In 1971 the tug was purchased by the Great Lakes Towing Company for intended use in Chicago. She received the GLT livery, but was never used. Sioux City got the tug back after a couple years and in 1980 Ed Barnaby purchased the twin screw tug and renamed it *Curly B*. After a couple years he repowered her with twin KTA-38-M Cummins producing a total of 1800-HP. The tug was sold to Joe Walsh, of Lake Michigan Contractors, in 1994 and it entered service on the Great Lakes as a dredge tug. She is spotted at LMC's Holland yard with her house down in September 1997.

On June 14, 1989, Barnaby's *Bonesey B.* has an Algoma Central ship on a tow line, bringing them up the Calumet River stern first. This canaller has a hull that is sort of a combination harbor tug/towboat design. Slightly squared off, it is intended for pushing barges and all other uses as well. It was built at Sturgeon Bay in 1974 for the Twin City Barge Lines as the *Donald O'Toole*. The well-known Material Service Corporation bought the tug in 1980 and kept it for six years before selling it to Calumet Marine Towing, who gave it the name she's wearing in this image. John Kindra bought out the Barnaby operation in the early 1990s and today she is operating as the *Morgan*. Upon purchase, Barnaby had removed her twin 12-645 EMDs and installed a pair of Cat 3512's. *Al Hart photo*

In 1924 the Manitowoc Tugboat Company ordered a new 86-foot harbor tug from Manitowoc Shipbuilding. It was launched the following year as their Hull No. 215 and named *Welcome*. She was powered by a recycled 24" x 26" 500-IHP steam engine which had been built in 1875 by Filer & Stowell at Milwaukee. This engine was actually salvaged from the *first* tugboat named *Welcome*, which was junked at Milwaukee in 1923. The newer *Welcome* was sold to Clark Towing in 1943, which later became part of Great Lakes Towing. The tug's cabin was rebuilt after conversion to diesel and a retractable pilothouse added for service in Chicago. She was given the state name *South Carolina* in 1972. Today the tug is powered by an EMD 12-567C and stationed at Burns Harbor with the *Massachusetts*.

Hannah's *Margaret M.* shoves the barge *Hannah 2901* up the Calumet River in South Chicago. The twin screw tug is powered by a pair of 12-cylinder D397 Caterpillars with 3.86:1 Twin Disc MG-527 reduction/reverse gears. The tug is well fitted, having a towing machine, facing winches, flanking rudders and a retractable pilothouse with a 17-foot lift. The tug was built in 1958 by Sturgeon Bay Shipbuilding as the *Shuttler*. It was renamed *Margaret M. Hannah* in 1960, a name which was shortened in 1984. *James Bartke photo*

Another Hannah canaller, the *Daryl C. Hannah*, is sandwiched in amongst her fleetmates in the 104th Street slip on December 20, 2002. The tug is a flat-fronted towboat for river service. It is named in honor of *Daryl Christine Hannah* (yes, the actress) and has been with the Hannah fleet since 1993. The low sleek tug can run the Chicago river systems and when needed, the pilothouse will rise an additional 25-feet on a hydraulic ram, to see up over her tow. The large push-knees on the bow are built into the hull and have sufficient strength for pushing multiple barges wired together. Winches on her bow are used to hook up to the tow.

The *Daryl C. Hannah* was locally built in 1956 at the Calumet Shipyard & Drydock Company for the Rose Barge Line as their *Cindy Jo*. The 102-footer is powered by two very interesting direct drive diesels. Pictured is her starboard engine, one of two 8-cylinder Superior model 40-M5X-8 engines. They are run through 3:1 Sea Master gears, although they are non-reversible. It has been said when maneuvering in tight quarters, one engine is run ahead while the other is run astern and her 2 steering rudders and 4 flanking rudders are used to control the movement of the tug, a set-up that apparently works quite well if you know what you're doing.